1995

those who wait for the Lord
  shall renew their strength,
they shall mount up with wings
  like eagles,
they shall run and not be weary,
  they shall walk and not faint.

Isaiah 40.31

I A N.

Dream the impossible
and make it happen.

    Love you always
      Aunt Barb.

THE JOURNEY

Stories and prayers for
the Christian year from
people of the First Nations

Edited by Joyce Carlson

Editorial Advisory Board
Alf Dumont, Laverne Jacobs,
Walter Jones, Stan McKay

Illustrated by Teresa Altiman

Readers
Andrew Atagotaluk, Phyllis Keeper,
Stan McKay Sr., Verna McKay,
Gladys Taylor, Murray Whetung

THE ANGLICAN BOOK CENTRE
Toronto, Canada

1991
Anglican Book Centre
600 Jarvis Street
Toronto, Ontario
Canada M4Y 2J6

Typesetting by Jay Tee Graphics Ltd.

Canadian Cataloguing in Publication Data

Main entry under title:

The Journey : stories and prayers for the Christian year from
    people of the First Nations

ISBN 0-921846-40-1

1. Church year meditations.   2. Prayer-books.
3. Indians of North America – Canada – Religion and
mythology. I. Carlson, Joyce.

BV30.J68 199   242'.3   C91-095543-3

Table of contents

Foreword

It is an honour for me to be asked to write some words about this splendid gathering of reflections on our faith through the witness of First Nation Christians.

The familiar adage about walking a mile in another's moccasins comes through forcefully here. Through the great Aboriginal tradition of story-telling we are privileged to share in the experience of others as we seek to understand more deeply how God works in the lives of all people and how we might more clearly be living our daily prayer ''Thy will be done.''

There are many ways this material can be used. It certainly can be part of personal reflection and meditation. Because it is connected to the lectionary readings, it can be used in oral or printed form either in church services or in church school classes, especially where a lectionary-based curriculum is the custom.

The first Native convocation hoped that First Nation congregations across the country might have more chance to hear the stories of their sisters and brothers elsewhere; *The Journey* gives a chance for many of those voices to be heard more widely.

Prayer groups and Bible study groups in the dominant society may want to take all or part of a year to consider the material as a means to hear how the gospel and the world connect for people in another culture which is geographically close but spiritually unfamiliar for many.

It is an honour to be a contributor to these stories because the Nisga'a people of British Columbia have given me a name and therefore a place inside the First Nations. And so I sign with that name.

K'al Wilimhlkws K'amligi Hahl Haahl
Primate of the Anglican Church of Canada

Acknowledgements

I travelled to many communities to collect stories for *The Journey*. I stayed at a residence overlooking Great Slave Lake, and watched the midsummer sun cast a pinking glow. Beside a sacred fire in Northern Manitoba, I felt a sudden summer storm. Over snowy hills in Echo Valley, Saskatchewan, I saw a winter sunrise.

I remember bright fireweed splashed along the McKenzie River and the flash of fur of drum dancers in Inuvik. I heard ravens cry from a fence at Fort McPherson. I visited a fishing hut nestled along the Peel River with purple mountains rising in the distance. I recall a bright spring day in Curve Lake, Ontario. I saw new leaves washed in rain at Anishinabe Centre near Sudbury.

I listened. I enjoyed the opportunity to hear stories over cups of tea at kitchen tables and in living rooms. I was welcomed in trust and friendship to meetings of leaders across Canada. Within communities, the circle of sharing is the circle of life. Often a story told by one person sparked a story by another. On paper we don't see the flow and life between the stories as we would in the storytelling circle. The stories, however, are closely related. In this sense, all persons present at meetings have shaped the book.

Storytelling requires a willingness to share of ourselves. This book reflects the deep trust of the storytelling circle. The advisory board is committed to publication to encourage the storytelling tradition, as well as to share more widely the teachings of Elders. It is our hope that readers will accept and respect the trust with which the stories were shared.

The meetings I attended in the United Church were: the annual meeting of the All Native Circle Conference in

Saddle Lake, Alberta (1989), the annual meeting in Nelson House, Manitoba (1990) as well as meetings with students at the Dr. Jessie Saulteaux Resource Centre. Within the Anglican Church, I attended: Council for Native Ministries in Anderson Lake (May 1990), Prairie Christian Training Centre in Saskatchewan (December 1990 and March 1988), National Executive Council in Winnipeg (May 1991) and Synod of the Arctic (July 1990).

Transcribed stories were edited in close consultation with storytellers. We are grateful to the following leaders who offered advice and encouragement: Andrew Atagotaluk, Pond Inlet; Phyllis Keeper, Winnipeg; Stan McKay Sr. and Verna McKay, Winnipeg; Gladys McCue Taylor, Curve Lake; and Murray Whetung, Curve Lake.

The Journey contains Inuit, Loucheaux, Cree, Assiniboine, Chippewa, Ojibwa, Cree, Oji-Cree, Blackfoot, Nisga'a and Gitsan stories. The story of Christ has entered a variety of cultures and is expressed in many voices, many experiences.

The challenge to present stories of an oral tradition in written form was approached with creativity by storytellers, by First Nations Ecumenical Liturgical Resources Board, and by Anglican Book Centre. *The Journey* is the result of a superb cooperative effort to communicate understandings of Christian faith for the benefit of First Nations communities as well as the larger Church.

The placement of stories was carefully reviewed by the editorial board. Following placement of stories with appropriate lectionary readings, prayers were composed for personal use as well as for possible incorporation into worship services.

Art by Teresa Altiman is a wonderful addition to the book. We are grateful to the Council for Native Ministries for their specific support to include her work.

The Diocese of the Arctic provided hospitality during Synod of the Arctic. Andy and Rachel Yorke welcomed me in their home in Fort McPherson. Thanks to Marilyn Perry for the opportunity to participate in editorial workshops with Wood Lake Books. Thanks to Bob Thomas whose understanding of computer technology speeded the project. For their help in xeroxing and faxing of materials I thank Cheryl Jourdain and Joanna Hart of the All Native Circle Conference.

Transcriptions of stories of Dr. Jessie Saulteaux are excerpted from an unpublished manuscript called "Morningstar." Stories by Sanadius Fiddler were also completed under the direction of the Dr. Jessie Saulteaux Resource Centre. These stories are published with the permission of the storytellers and the Dr. Jessie Saulteaux Resource Centre. I am indebted to the staff of the Centre: Raphaela Johnston, John McFarlane, Janet Silman, Leyah McFadyen and Stan McKay for their encouragement.

A special note of appreciation is due my husband, Len, and children, Karen, Andrea and Ian. Their support over two years permitted my involvement in the project. Families of First Nations Ecumenical Liturgical Resources Board: Dorothy McKay, Daniel and Becky; Lynn Jacobs and Charlie; Barb Dumont, Michael and Daniel; and Marilyn Jones, are also to be thanked for their patience. The high commitment of the advisory board called for long meetings added to busy schedules.

It is our hope that *The Journey* will encourage more sharing of stories and prayers.

Joyce Carlson
Editor

Persons whose stories appear in this resource are: Evelyn Broadfoot, Laverne Jacobs, Percy Henry, Art Anderson, Jessie Saulteaux, Andrew Atagotaluk, Sanadius Fiddler, Gladys McCue Taylor, Phyllis Keeper, Murray Whetung, Stan McKay, Caleb Lawrence, Clara Tizya, Redfern Loutit, Margaret Waterchief, James Isbister, Benjamin Wood, Michael Peers, Daniel Aupalu, Lana Grawbarger, Sarah Simon, William Dumas, Walter Jones, Meeka Arnakak, Alf Dumont, Johnston Garrioch, Samuel Bull, Vi Smith, Edith Memnook, Monica McKay, and David Masty.

All stories are used by permission of the storytellers.

Preparation of materials for this ecumenical resource was made possible through grants from:

The Isabel Johnson Bequest Fund, Anglican Church of Canada
The Division of Mission in Canada, United Church of Canada
The St. Stephen's Broadway Foundation of Winnipeg, United Church of Canada
Diocese of Rupert's Land, Anglican Church of Canada
Council for Native Ministries, Anglican Church of Canada
Resource Development, United Church of Canada

THE SEASON OF ADVENT

*Look up and raise your heads,
because your redemption is drawing
near.*

Luke 21:28

FIRST SUNDAY OF ADVENT

Look up and raise your heads, because your redemption is drawing near. *Luke 21.28*

Readings
Jeremiah 33.14–16   *Psalm 25.1–9*
1 Thessalonians 3.9–13   *Luke 21.25–36*

I was born in Norway House.

When I was seven years old I lost my mother. I was the baby of the family for seven years and then my sister came along. My mother died when my sister was two weeks old.

When I think back I feel I was lucky because I understand that God speaks to little children wherever they are.

My mother died in the summer. The next spring my father went out on the trapline and took the whole family with him. We all had jobs to do while we were out on the trapline. My sister and I had the job of getting water for washing or making tea.

For some reason my sister couldn't go one day, so I went down to the river by myself to get water.

I took a teapot and ran down to the river. I felt that I needed to sit down before getting water.

It was a beautiful day, and the river was just like glass. Something happened as I sat there, something came over me. It was like the wind, a warm wind — I didn't know what it was but it felt good.

I got up and got the water and went running up with it. I didn't tell anyone — but I knew there was a God.

My father used to come and wake us up in the morning, "Look outside," he'd say, "listen to the birds!" "Don't lie in bed too long because God, Gitchie Manitou is here."

When I had that experience, I knew there was a God. Ever since, I have always felt there was a God. I have tried to deny the existence of God — I have tried to go on my own and put aside His teachings. But I have always come back and I feel now what a privilege I have had to have parents who cared enough to talk of the good things and teach me of God.

Evelyn Broadfoot
White Bear, Saskatchewan/
Norway House, Manitoba

Prayer for meditation
Lord,
you come to us in the quiet of the day.
You come in the sun rising pink in the morning sky
and shining on the calm waters of a river.
In our times of trouble when we suffer loss and despair,
Lord, come.

Prayer for all people
That God's love in us may make us generous in love, in loving one another and the whole human race, let us pray to the Lord.

SECOND SUNDAY OF ADVENT

Prepare the way of the Lord, make his paths straight. All flesh shall see the salvation of God. *Luke 3.4, 6*

Readings
Malachi 3.1–4   *Psalm 126*
Philippians 1.3–11   *Luke 3.1–6*

When I was a child, I was very much alone. Because of ill health, I had to spend much time in the hospital; so I was by myself and separated from my family. I was a premature child and I was always rather frail. I remember my mother saying that she had prayed that I would live. There were times when it was feared I would not make it.

There were many times when I went outside and my mother had to put me on a blanket by myself because I couldn't run and play as my brothers and sisters did. I remember looking at them and wishing I could be like that, wishing I could run and play like the others.

Years later, I was sitting in a university one day and someone said to me, ''I wish that I had what you have.'' I wondered at that time what that would be. Now I think I understand that out of my physical weakness there has grown a strength. It is a sense of quietness, of being able to be still.

Many people see this as a quiet strength. I had to spend a great deal of time by myself and I learned to be by myself. Our family was upheld by our faith in God — and that is why the hymns and the Scriptures mean so much to me. The symbol of the cross means so much to me. It was faith which allowed me to live and pulled me through and gave me strength.

An important influence in my life was my grandmother. My grandmother was an invalid as long as I can remember. She was hardly able to move at all — but many people came to her. She was able to do an incredible ministry to so many in our community. Many, many people came to her and she was a very spiritual person. I remember sitting by her bed many times. I remember how much impact her faith had on the lives of others in spite of her illness.

I believe I have a gift of enabling others and assisting

others to find their own gifts and to use them. I think this comes out of the long struggle I have had with illness and the need in my early life to be adjusted to the isolation I sometimes felt. I find that it is something I am able to see now as a strength — and it may enable others in their growth in faith.

Laverne Jacobs
Oakville/Walpole Island,
Ontario

Prayer for meditation
Creator God,
we come to you as children,
looking out into the world from our own places.

May we be open to the message of good news in our lives, may we nurture a place where your love may grow.

We give thanks for the witness of your faithful servants who inspire your love to grow in us.

Prayer for all people
That the love of the Creator may overflow more and more in us so that in the day of Christ, we may be pure and blameless, having produced the harvest of righteousness that comes through Jesus Christ, let us pray to the Lord.

THIRD SUNDAY OF ADVENT

The Spirit of the Lord God is upon me, because the Lord has anointed me to bring good tidings to the afflicted.
Isaiah 61.1

ADVENT

Readings

Zephaniah 3.14–20
Philippians 4.4–9
Luke 3.7–18

Canticle 3, Song of
Thanksgiving
(Isaiah 12.2–6)

When my youngest boy died, the one that I cherished, I cried. I wanted a drink so bad, I could even taste the booze — but I quit drinking eight years ago. My boy four years ago said no matter what happens, don't drink dad, don't ever drink again. So I asked God for strength.

My son was out working on the car. He came into the house, poured coffee, hugged his mom and said, "I'm sorry mom." And he went into his bedroom and committed suicide at 4:20 p.m.

When my daughter drowned on 31 July 1982, I was also chief at the time and I went out looking for her body from the day it happened until September. On the last day, when the ice was forming, I saw water flowing in two directions and it was like a sign from heaven. I said, "Lord, you've given me a job — now help me to do it."

I am not the only one with problems — We drop our young people like hot potatoes. I see that now. They go to the white man's school and all they get are promises. They come back to us and they don't make sense to us.

My mother and dad are still living. They are sixty-six years married and now they start to tell me things. They say, "You've got to learn these things."

I say, "It's a fine time to tell me now!"

Many Elders who could help us have died. When we first got mixed up with the white man in 1954, the Elders died like flies. They froze to death, many of them from the alcohol.

19

I stopped drinking before my wife and she used to give me a rough time. She said I didn't care or I didn't love her.

I started to trust her and all the bad feeling went away. She tried to argue and I said, "Let's talk about it first." After a while she stopped arguing; there was nothing to argue about.

"How did you do it?" she asked.

"Only one person can do it and that's you," I said. "You have a spirit and God knows that spirit. God will work with that spirit. If I interfere and start fooling with that, I might ruin you for life."

She's been sober four years.

God says, "trust me." It's hard but I still try to be happy.

Percy Henry
Dawson City/Hart River,
Yukon

Prayer for meditation
Lord,
in our weakness we reach out to you.
Oh, for a glimpse of your love!

We look for you, Lord.
When we cannot trust ourselves,
we trust in your strength to guide our hearts.

Grant us forgiveness and grace.

Prayer for all people
That the peace of God, which surpasses all understanding will guard our hearts and minds in Christ Jesus, let us pray to the Lord.

FOURTH SUNDAY OF ADVENT

I am the servant of the Lord; let it be to me according to his word. *Luke 1.38*

Readings
Micah 5.2–4   *Psalm 80.1–7*
Hebrews 10.5–10   *Luke 1.39–55*

I am a father of two boys who committed suicide.

In 1968, I was asked to be chief. There had been no chief in Dawson for twenty-five years. Twenty-five years without a leader!

When I went to a meeting to elect a chief, I found I was elected. I didn't know about Indian Affairs or the Indian Agent. I asked God if that's what I should be doing: I asked for help. I went to meetings and got involved in land claims. My kids would say, "Hi dad" and, "Bye dad." I was hardly ever home — I was just coming and going.

Later on, I was elected to Elder Council and Chief of the Yukon. When I went to the meeting, I found the youngest was seventy years old. I asked if I could resign.

An Elder got up and said I could resign if I could prove that I was getting younger.

So I was stuck there — and I'm still stuck there. I went to meetings across Canada. I heard the Elders say God is calling the Indian people back together. We are to prepare ourselves.

When I was a kid I worked for the old people to hear their stories. As chief, I have many young people come to me to ask about the old religion, our old traditions.

They think the chief should know everything.

I went to an Elder lady who is about one hundred and twenty years old. She is very smart and could tell me so many things. She said that our Elders were responsible for teaching how Elders should act, and how parents should act and how to care for everything and the country we live on.

She remembered when Bishop McDonald came up the Mackenzie River — the elder people would walk once a year three or four hundred miles just to get Holy Communion once a year.

I once went over that land in a helicopter; it was rough land and they went over it on foot and with canoes.

"Today," she said, "we have churches on sidewalks, and no-one can seem to walk across the sidewalk to the church!" We have to listen to the Elders; they can see far ahead.

What I thought was impossible is starting to happen. What I see today is we're coming together as a people.

This is a start; we have to keep on going for the sake of our young people.

Percy Henry
Dawson City/Hart River,
Yukon

Prayer for meditation
Restore us, O Lord,
let your face shine upon us,
and grant us your peace.

We wait in expectation
for the fulfilment of your promise to us, your people.

Fill us with good things,
help us over rough ground
to the place of your love and mercy.

Prayer for all people

That we may understand the profound truth that we have been sanctified through the offering of the body of Jesus Christ once for all, let us pray to the Lord.

THE SEASON OF CHRISTMAS

*I bring you good news of great joy
which will come to all the people;
for to you is born this day a Saviour,
Christ the Lord.*

Luke 2.10–11

CHRISTMAS — AT MIDNIGHT

I bring you good news of great joy which will come to all the people; for to you is born this day a Saviour, Christ the Lord. *Luke 2.10–11*

Readings
Isaiah 9.2–7   *Psalm 96*
Titus 2.11–14   *Luke 2.1–20*

My dad was in the trenches in France in World War One.* One Christmas Eve he was on guard duty. There was a great space called "no man's land" lying between the German Army and the Canadian Army.

It was very quiet on the front. All the officers were pulled out from the front and were back somewhere having their Christmas dinners. There was only the ordinary soldiers up front in the trenches.

He looked up. He saw a cloud formation — and the clouds were in the form of angels. He found himself humming a Christmas carol. Then, the next man took it up — and the next and the next until all along the Canadian line from out of the trenches there was the sound of "Silent Night" being sung. Suddenly, there was the sound of the same hymn being sung by the Germans from their side of the trenches and in their own language.

Then, some of the guys started going out. Pretty soon everyone was out in the middle of no man's land. They didn't have very much to give to each other — but they gave what they could, a piece of chocolate, or a cigarette is all they had — and they gave these gifts to each other.

---

* Art Anderson's father hated residential school. He ran away from the school at the age of sixteen and joined the Canadian Armed Forces. It was during this time that he had the experience recorded here. Many young men from reserves across Canada were involved in both the First and Second World Wars.

My father still remembers it clearly; the angels hovering over, the singing together, one side in English, one side in German — and the exchange of gifts out there in no man's land.

Art Anderson
Regina/Kāneonuskatēw* (Gordon's Reserve),
Saskatchewan

* Kāneonuskatēw translated in English is "one that walks on four claws."

Prayer for meditation
Lord God,
Creator of heaven and earth,
your love stretches over dark places,
and reaches into the no man's land of our lives,
the place where hope, goodness and truth no longer live.

There, you announce your child.
When we see that truth, we give thanks,
reaching out to each other in reconciliation,
planting the seeds of new life.

Grant us the courage to look up
to see your angels rising before us,
bringing the promise of new life.

Grant us the grace to seek the Christ child,
that we may offer our gifts to him.

Prayer for all people
That the grace of God which has appeared may bring salvation to all and that we may live lives that are upright and godly while we wait for the blessed hope and the manifestation of the glory of our great God and Saviour, Jesus Christ, let us pray to the Lord.

CHRISTMAS — DURING THE DAY

I bring you good news of great joy which will come to all the people; for to you is born this day a Saviour, Christ the Lord. *Luke 2.10–11*

Readings
Isaiah 9.2–7   Psalm 96
Titus 2.11–14   Luke 2.1–20

I was sent to the residential school at Sioux Lookout when I was seven years old. I don't remember very much of my first two to three years at the school, perhaps because most of the memories would not be very pleasant.

I remember very clearly however being marched into the dining room one evening after supper. This happened during my third year at the school. I was wondering what we had done wrong as the only time we were taken into the dining room in these circumstances was to be "bawled out" about something we had or had not done, or to be questioned about something that the staff were investigating. If nobody spoke up, confessed, or "squeeled on" someone else, we had to stand up for hours. If no-one said anything we were made to stand for three evenings, for two to three hours each evening.

This particular evening, I was surprised to see a man in a red suit with a big white beard. I had never seen Santa Claus before. We were given one candy cane and a book. I had not yet learned to read and only understood a little English. The books they gave us weren't children's books. I don't remember what happened to those books.

We each were given one cookie and some kind of fruit juice. It was the first time we had ever been given fruit juice. After we went upstairs, one of the girls gave me a wrapped present. It was one of her dresses that I had admired. I was so happy because I knew we were allowed to wear our own clothes on Christmas day. The next day I put on the dress and was very surprised when one of the supervisors started yelling at me. I didn't understand what she was saying except the word steal. I had often heard the kids say that they were going to steal bread because they were hungry.

The supervisor was accusing me of stealing the dress and the girl who had given it to me couldn't say anything as the kids were not allowed to give each other presents.

As a special treat for Christmas supper the children were given some candies and nuts, and one orange. I didn't get the treats. I had to scrub stairs and go right to bed. Scrubbing the stairs was a terrible punishment because the stairs were concrete and we had to scrub them in our bare feet using lye soap. After I finished, I was all alone in the big dormitory and I remember taking off the back of the toilet and trying to wash my hands in the water there. I was afraid to go downstairs or to turn on the light in the dormitory.

After the girls came to bed and the lights were out, Jessie, the girl who had given me the present, felt so bad about getting me into trouble that she came over to my bed and gave me half an orange and candies. Some of the other girls shared their treats with me. Soon I had more than they had, and I was able to share with some of the smaller kids. Jessie became a very good friend.

I'll never forget. That was so nice to have her share what she had. We were so happy that we just cried together. We were hit if we were found crying — but we couldn't help ourselves. It was so beautiful, that moment. We had such deep feelings.

I believe that this experience was a very good one for me. It taught me the importance of sharing not only food and material things but also the importance of sharing feelings of love and caring. It showed me how a bad experience can become a good experience when we share and care for one another. It is something God taught me at that time through the love and sharing of my friends in the school.

Phyllis Keeper
Winnipeg, Manitoba/
Big Trout Lake, Ontario

Prayer for meditation
Lord God,
Creator of heaven and earth,
your love stretches everywhere,
reaching into the hearts of children
when all seems desolate and empty.

We give thanks for your love.
We give thanks for the joy of children in spontaneous sharing,
caring for each other and bringing reconciliation and love.
In their innocence they bring the promise of new life.

Grant us the grace to seek the Christ child,
in everything that we do, in everyone that we meet.

May we offer our gifts to him.

Prayer for all people
That we may live lives that are upright and godly while we wait for the blessed hope and the manifestation of the glory of our great God and Saviour, Jesus Christ, let us pray to the Lord.

FIRST SUNDAY AFTER CHRISTMAS

Let the peace of Christ rule in your hearts; let the word of Christ dwell in you richly. *Colossians 3.15, 16*

Readings

1 Samuel 2.18–20, 26 or   Psalm 111
   Sirach 3.3–7, 14–17   Luke 2.41–52
Colossians 3.12–17

In recent years, many people in our communities have joined settlements. My own father and mother did not do this — and I respect them for it. They felt it important to stay with their own way of life. They still live on the land and make their living by the land.

I went out of their camp to have an education. For me, education was a good experience. I always thought that once I had finished my education, I would go back and become a hunter like my father.

My father was a very good hunter.

When people think of hunting, they think of going out and seeing an animal and shooting right away. But that is not how the Inuit have hunted. I remember when I went out with my father and watched him hunt.

If he saw a group of five or six caribou, he would watch them very quietly. He would watch for hours without ever making a sound. After a while, he would know from the way the animals were behaving which animal was the leader. When everything was right, he would shoot the leader of the group. Immediately after the first shot the whole herd is startled, but, without their leader, they would not know which way to run or what to do. By being patient in this way, a good hunter would have perhaps three or four animals before they could escape.

If he had seen the herd and shot immediately without knowing which was the leader, the leader would have sprung up and led the others to safety. This is why it is important to understand the animals and the land. In the old days, understanding these matters meant the difference between survival and starvation of the family.

I was translating the Bible into the Inuit language when I began to understand what the words of Jesus meant.

In our communities there are many who are lost. There has been a disruption of the old way of life and the new way is not yet adjusted to. It is hard to describe, but when you move to a settlement and live in a house — there are many things which are new and different and the people do not know how to live with the differences.

The language has almost completely gone in some communities. The things of their own culture are gone and the pride in their own accomplishments and what they might do is also gone.

Life can be very rough sometimes — in part because one does not know how to anticipate what the changes will be. For example, a television causes great change. It used to be that people would visit with each other and they would spend time in getting to know each other. Now, there is very little visiting. People live separately rather than in groups where they would be sharing more of life. Watching television changes the way we are.

Knowing Christ calls me to retain my own culture, traditions and language. Christ calls me to more fullness of life and that means to take pride in myself as an Inuit person. This is what I share with people when I talk to them about Christ and what it means to be a Christian. With all the changes that are happening in our communities in the North this is important. I know that I myself would not know what to do and what way to follow if I were not a follower of Christ.

I always thought that I would go back to the land and be a

hunter like my father. But, I couldn't go back. Instead, I am a priest serving my people.

Andrew Atagotaluk
Pond Inlet,
Northwest Territories

Prayer for meditation
Creator God,
as the things of the past are gone,
we struggle to understand what we must do, how we must live.

Your word is an anchor in the midst of change,
your teaching guides us into a new future.

May we find ways to serve each other in your love.
As God's chosen people may we clothe ourselves
with compassion, kindness, humility, meekness, and patience,
bearing with one another and forgiving one another.

Prayer for all people
That the peace of Christ may rule in our hearts and the word of Christ dwell in us, teaching us in all wisdom that we may, with gratitude in our hearts, sing to God, let us pray to the Lord.

THE NAMING OF JESUS — *1 January*

God spoke of old by the prophets; but in these last days he has spoken to us by a Son. *Hebrews 1.1–2*

Readings
Numbers 6.22–27   *Psalm 67*
Galatians 4.4–7 or Philippians 2.9–13   *Luke 2.15–21*

In our culture, we're taught that when a new baby comes, the baby is baptized in the church. Then there is a new-born baby feast at the home of the parents.

To begin the feast for celebration of the baby's birth, the Elders hold and talk to the baby. The baby is told that God has sent him/her to live and to work on the earth. The baby is told how hard life is, how rough it is — the evil things that must be 'gone through.

After that, a child is given an Indian name. The Indian name is different from the name given at baptism. Parents usually give an English name at the time of baptism.

We usually ask an Elder to give the baby the Indian name. The Elder is a trusted and wise person who will take a special interest in the child.

Naming must be done in the home of the person who is naming the baby. We each bring some food along for the man or woman who is naming the baby.

To name the child, one must be seated on the floor, to remind us we must be close to the earth. A long time ago there were no floors, only bare ground — and so we really were on the earth. A cloth or blanket is spread on the floor and the food is spread on the cloth. Everyone is seated in a circle around the feast.

The baby is given the Indian name to carry throughout life. The child is taught to respect the name which is given to him/her. The namer always remembers the name of the child. When the naming is done, the baby is handed back to the mother. The mother passes the child along to each person gathered in the circle, and each person says the baby's name and kisses the baby, welcoming it into the community.

Not many actually use the Indian name — but they keep it.

Some people forget their Indian name — especially now that the culture is being lost. But some go on to use their Indian names — sometimes much later in their lives they come to be known by that name.

Then, the Sacred Pipe is lit and handed around the circle, each person taking a puff in turn. A prayer is said — and a grace. Then food and tea are taken.

Sanadius Fiddler
Sandy Lake, Ontario

Prayer for meditation
Creator God,
you have given your Son the name above every name.

May we remember always that through the spirit
of your Son
in our hearts we are heirs to your eternal kingdom.

You have known us since before we were conceived.
May we understand it is you at work in us
enabling us to work for your good pleasure,
so that we may be your children in our generation,
shining like stars in the world.

We give thanks for celebrations
reminding us of who we are as people,
and welcoming us into the community of God.

Prayer for all people
That we may live out our faith in true freedom, working for good in our own communities as God would have us do, let us pray to the Lord.

SECOND SUNDAY OF CHRISTMAS

Glory to Christ who is preached among the nations, and believed on in the world. *See 1 Timothy 3.16*

Readings
Jeremiah 31.7–14 or
   Sirach 24.1–4, 12–16
Ephesians 1.3–6, 15–18

Psalm 147.13–21
John 1.1–18

When I first learned how to read, I was so happy and excited that I ran straight home to my dad. "I can read!" I cried.

He replied, "That is very good." He stood beside me as I brought out my book to read. Standing tall as I had been taught, I haltingly began *The Little Red Hen*. It wasn't a long or difficult book — but it took me a very long time. When I had finished my father said, "That was very good — I am very proud of you."

I was so happy in that moment. As I held the book with my dad standing beside me, his hand on my shoulder, I felt that he and I were standing on the rim of a silver circle. Through the centre of the circle we were seeing a completely strange and different world — a world where different people thought, talked, and lived in a different way. I knew, too, that I was going to have to learn to live in that world.

My own language is the language of my heart; it is the language I use when I pray. I was punished in school for speaking my own language. I never learned to write in my own language.

It seemed to me that I held two separate containers inside myself. On one side I held my own language, and on the other side the language of communication with the outside world. The separate containers didn't match. The Ojibwa language and the English language are different. It was always hard to translate one into the other, because words meant different things in each language. Sometimes it seemed as though these two parts of myself were fighting.

It was very painful, but I found that out of that struggle came a spring of living water. It was the storytelling flowing from deep inside me. I speak from my heart. When we speak from our hearts, we find ways to understand each other — although we might speak different languages.

When I think about different traditions, I think about that silver circle, how my father and I stood so long ago and looked into the different world on the pages.

The circle is the circle of life and the Creator is at the centre of the circle. Different ways can meet. These things can come together.

If we keep our eyes on the Creator, we will find ourselves able to respect each other in the different cultures — and in our own cultures — when we have differences.

Gladys Taylor
Curve Lake, Ontario

Prayer for meditation
Creator God,
the Word became flesh and lived among us,
full of grace and truth.

To all who receive your Son,
you give power to become your children.
We give thanks for transformations —
for a child's struggle to understand different worlds,
for the rich gift of storytelling arising from the struggle.

Lord, to you we lift up our souls,
in you we trust; teach us your ways
and lead us into all truth.

Prayer for all people

That the God of our Lord Jesus Christ may give us a spirit of wisdom and revelation, so that we may know the hope he has called us to, the riches of his inheritance, and the greatness of his power, let us pray to the Lord.

THE SEASON OF
THE EPIPHANY

*We have seen his star in the
East and have come to worship
him.*

Matthew 2.2

THE EPIPHANY — *6 January*

We have seen his star in the East, and have come to worship him. *Matthew 2.2*

Readings
Isaiah 60.1–6   *Psalm 72:1–14*
Ephesians 3.1–12   *Matthew 2.1–12*

My father and grandfather were both ministers.

When I was very young, my grandfather preached a sermon.

He said that there were strangers arriving — and that each person in our community should take something to greet the people so they would not have to cook on the day of their arrival when they would be tired and hungry.

He said this was out of courtesy and respect for the people he knew would be exhausted from their journey.

I loved and admired my grandfather so much. I ran straight home from church. The roast was in the oven — and I ran with it as fast as I could and gave it to the people who were arriving.

My grandmother was much slower in coming home. When she came and found that the meal for the family was gone, she was very angry.

I could see my grandfather moving close to her and nudging her with his elbow. I could hear him saying, "We can't be angry at Phyllis. This is what I preached about this morning. This is how we are teaching her. She is only following what we are teaching her."

Phyllis Keeper
Winnipeg, Manitoba/
Big Trout Lake, Ontario

Prayer for meditation

Creator,
you came to us a child,
an infant born in a stable.

May we open our eyes,
and see you anew everywhere we are, in everything
we do.

Prayer for all people

That the mystery of Christ made known to humankind may
bring us all to share in the promise in Christ Jesus through
the gospel, let us pray to the Lord.

THE BAPTISM OF THE LORD or THE FIRST SUNDAY AFTER EPIPHANY

A voice came from heaven, saying, ''This is my beloved
Son with whom I am well pleased.'' *Matthew 3.17*

Readings

Isaiah 61.1–4   *Psalm 29*
Acts 8.14–17   *Luke 3:15–17, 21–22*

As a child I never liked my name. The name Phyllis is very
difficult to pronounce in the Cree and Ojibwa languages as
the sound *f* is not used. It was an uncommon name in my
community.

I grew to like my name only after my parents told me why
I had received it. My parents had not yet named me when
a young pilot came to our community.

They were having a feast when the pilot asked what was
happening. He was told that a feast was being held to

43

celebrate the birth of a health baby girl. My mother explained that they were having a feast and giving thanks to God as my parents had lost two babies between me and my oldest brother.

The pilot asked my family if they had named me yet. When they said they had not, the pilot asked them to name me Phyllis in memory of his wife who had recently died and whose name was Phyllis. My parents agreed and so my name is Phyllis.

My parents told me that, every time he came, he would bring a present and hold me in his arms. He became friends with people in our community. He earned their respect because he was a kind and honest man. They learned to say my name out of respect for him.

When I went to the residential school, the supervisor said that in the thirty years she had worked with Indian children she had never heard the name Phyllis until I came along.

My parents also told me that actually they had planned to call me Madeline after my mother. Madeline is my second name.

Phyllis Keeper
Winnipeg, Manitoba/
Big Trout Lake, Ontario

Prayer for meditation
Creator,
your Spirit came
to proclaim liberty to the captives,
release to the prisoners.

Grant us strength and grace to welcome strangers,
to comfort those who mourn.

Prayer for all people

That all may receive the word of God and be blessed with understanding of his love and peace, let us pray to the Lord.

SECOND SUNDAY AFTER EPIPHANY

Jesus manifested his glory, and his disciples believed in him. *John 2.11*

Readings

Isaiah 62.1–5   Psalm 36.5–10

1 Corinthians 12.1–11   John 2.1–11

When people tell the stories of their struggles, it is helpful. Then they are able to leave these things behind. We have to leave behind those things that are destroying us. We have to leave those things behind.

I remember a time when we went to Presbytery and they would tell us what they were going to do.

Aboriginal people believed that they could handle their own affairs. Aboriginal people knew and understood that when they talked about religion, they talked with respect. There is a difference between the evangelical zeal of the Church — and the longhouse tradition.

In the longhouse tradition, when one spoke to another, one spoke with respect. Aboriginal people found that when they went into the Church, people sometimes started arguing. They didn't respect each other. Instead, they put others down.

This has been a source of confusion for people. In our own

45

worship we sing hymns and have ceremonies and Bible readings.

At the formation of our own Presbyteries we are small in number. But although we are small in number and often struggle, we are aware we are still better off than sitting at the back of the room waiting for others to tell us what they are going to do.

We may still struggle — but we are doing it ourselves.

Stan McKay
Winnipeg/Fisher River,
Manitoba

Prayer for meditation
Dear God, we thank you for being our own God,
for each beautiful morning,
and we ask that you continue to bless us.
We ask this in your name.

Murray Whetung
Curve Lake, Ontario

Creator God,
you are faithful, righteous, and just.
We take refuge in the shadow of your wings,
and find in you the fountain of all life.
You have given us gifts by which we may serve you.
May we rejoice in those gifts.

Prayer for all people
That the variety of gifts within our communities may be uncovered and recovered that we may work to the common good of all, let us pray to the Lord.

THIRD SUNDAY AFTER EPIPHANY

The Lord has anointed me to preach good news to the poor and release to the captives. *Luke 4.18*

Readings
Nehemiah 8.1–4a, 5–6, 8–10   Psalm 19.7–14
1 Corinthians 12.12–30   Luke 4.14–21

There is a word in Cree* which is used to translate the word "peace." When I was able to understand the root meaning of this word from the Elders as I was learning the Cree dialect, I could not help but think how beautiful it was and how theologically appropriate and descriptive. Their word for "peace" is a description of the moment in the spring when after a rain, all is fresh and green as the sun emerges. It is as though in the calm and beauty of the moment, all of creation is gathering its forces to surge forward to grow, blossom and push towards fruition with the single focus of becoming all it was meant to be. The world is filled with new life and song bringing delight and joy to the Creator and all God's people. That is "peace" from the perspective of the Cree language.

Caleb Lawrence
Schumacher, Ontario

Prayer for meditation
Creator,
in the days of your prophets,
your word was heard with respect
and the joy of the Lord was the strength of the people.

---

* The root word for peace is *chiyam*, but when used in services, a longer form of the word is used, the longer form is *chiyamayitamowin*.

In our time,
we know that joy in our lives.
We give thanks that your truth
which we understand from your word
is to be used in the healing of our families and
communities.

As we continue the journey,
struggling in our own ways and with our own understandings
may we hold ever before us the vision of ''peace''
brought to us by the Elders.

Prayer for all people
That there may be no divisions among us, but that we may
be united in the same mind and with the same purpose, let
us pray to the Lord.

FOURTH SUNDAY AFTER EPIPHANY

The Lord has anointed me to preach good news to the
poor and release to the captives. *Luke 4.18*

Readings
Jeremiah 1.4–10   Psalm 71.1–6
1 Corinthians 13.1–13   Luke 4.21–30

I went to C.G.I.T. and to Mission Band and to Sunday
School. It seemed always I would become president of one
or another of these groups. Here, I got experience about
leadership. Here, I also got to know a girl from grade eight
who wanted to go into nursing — and they got her to go
to St. Boniface — but she had to go in as a French girl
because they didn't accept Indians at that time.

When I finished grade eight, I couldn't go back to Round Lake School. They told me if I wanted to stay I could work in the school laundry. If I wanted to continue school, I could go on to another school. They told me to go home and think about it over the holiday. I thought about this and decided to go to Brandon. I wanted to take nursing and thought this would be a way to go into it. But, I got sick before I finished grade nine. I was eighteen then. The school had sheep — and the sheep were killed for meat. I was not used to the meat of the sheep — and they gave us the grease from sheep instead of butter on our bread. The principal arranged for me to take separate food and it helped. They didn't expect me to take exams — but I did take the exams. I passed, although I never went back. By that time I found out that I was too much of an Indian; I was too dark to be accepted into nursing. When I knew I wasn't going to be accepted in training or in a job, I came back to the reserve.

With two brothers and my sister and the other young people my age, I tried to see what we could do on the reserve. We had basket socials and dances. We had hockey games and skating wherever there was a good slough.* Whatever we could round up and organize, we did.

In those days, the Y.M.C.A. was quite strong on the reserve and they trained local leadership. Around 1925 to 1932 they came to the reserve — and they had a few meetings with the men. From then, the men carried on and they used to take turns holding services, even for funerals. They had a minister who used to come once a month, and the minister did the marriages. Later on, when the other denominations took over, the Y.M.C.A. and the local leadership died off.

---

* A *slough* is low land with water lying in it.

I think now there are too many denominations. The ''Y''
was good; they trained the local leadership. We had hymns
in our own language with them. They were really active in
those days when I was in Round Lake School.

Jessie Saulteaux
Carry the Kettle,
Saskatchewan

Prayer for meditation
Creator God,
you have known us from before we were born.
We are yours.

Sometimes when we hear your call,
it seems that all doors are closed —
but in the hearts of your people your word takes hold,
and calls us to work in faith in whatever ways we are able
to bring new life, healing, and hope.

We give thanks for the vision and example
of those who in spite of all obstacles
continue to exercise leadership.

Prayer for all people
That our love may ever increase as our understanding of
your word and intention for us grows, let us pray to the
Lord.

Dr. Jessie Saulteaux is an Elder whose life was spent in commitment to
finding ways to encourage local leadership within Native communities.
The Dr. Jessie Saulteaux Resource Centre, the first Aboriginal Theological
Centre in the United Church of Canada with an Aboriginal Board, was so
named to honour her lifetime support of local leadership training.

FIFTH SUNDAY AFTER EPIPHANY

I am the light of the world, says the Lord. Those who follow me will not walk in darkness, but will have the light of life. *John 8.12*

Readings
Isaiah 61.1–8 (9–13)   *Psalm 138*
1 Corinthians 15.1–11   *Luke 5.1–11*

As I grew up, I had a lot of questions about my life: Why was I premature when I was born? Why was I the littlest one in the class? Why was I sick all the time? I spent a lot of time in hospitals. I remember as a nine-year-old child, going into the nursing station and being taken by the doctor a long, long way away and being put into the hospital. I remember one time I was in bed and I wasn't allowed out of it. The nurses didn't really understand children. I wanted to get up, to do something — anything — to help make the bed. They put me right back in bed.

The nurse said, "You can't move." My heart was beating too fast and they were trying to regulate it. I went through so much of that. When that kind of illness happens, you ask a lot of questions — and I guess I was asking — Why?

Those are the physical things I struggled with. When I was young there was a lot of alcoholism on the reserve. I used to feel so ashamed sometimes. There were buses from Wallaceburg to my reserve. If you took the last bus home from Wallaceburg to the reserve, it was quite an experience. People were just plastered. I was so ashamed of being Indian.

I remember riding home on one of those buses and being so ashamed of being a part of those people who were so stoned out of their minds and didn't know what they were doing. You would see them around town — people leaning around buildings, or on lamp-posts. It didn't feel good as a teenager to have to put up with that. I wanted out.

My mom went to high school and on to teacher's college, and dad had a grade-twelve education. They wanted something better for us. When I look back, I realize the amount of sacrifice that they made. I remember the one time that my mother had a new dress. I don't know what she did the rest of the time, but I know that this was the only time that I remember she had a new dress. At other times, she must have just had things handed down or bought at rummage sales. In all of that — that one new dress stands out.

In all of those circumstances, I guess there was a motivation that encouraged me to want to grow up to be a doctor — or to help young people. Then I thought — I could be a minister. I don't know how — but I ended up thinking I could be a minister.

I valued education, but my motives to get an education were very mixed. I wanted somehow to help my people. I also wanted to run away — to run away and not go back. It was just too painful. But God had his way of dealing with some very difficult things. When I was in grade thirteen, I did very well at Christmas. I had an 85-per cent average.

That year my dad was running for chief. There were some political dynamics going on at the reserve which really affected me. In June, I really bombed out and I failed my year. I really felt broken. I remember sitting at the kitchen table, crying, and saying, "I'm going to be stuck on the reserve; I'm just going to be like everybody else." My mother placed her arms around me and was just there beside me. I was having to come to grips with "this may be my lot and learn to accept this." I had to work through that. And the failure was not graduating, not being able to go on — and not going into the ministry. I thought maybe ministry was not where God wanted me to be — and I had to relinquish that vision.

I applied for a job in a local bank. I wrote the aptitude test and apparently did very well. Unknown to me, our pastor went to the bank manager saying, "I understand Laverne applied for a job here . . . are you going to hire him?" The bank manager said, "No, because he's Indian." The minister said, "Well, you'd better think about that." I didn't know that this had happened. In the end I was hired . . . and I began to work in the bank. I was the first Native person to work in a bank in Wallaceburg. That meant a great deal. It meant a great deal to me and my people in Walpole. It also gave the people in the neighbouring town the opportunity to experience a Native person in a different way.

After a couple of weeks, church officials came to me saying, "We can get you into university — are you going to go?" I said, "No" . . . because I knew if I quit after a couple of weeks that I would only reinforce the negative image of Indians. After two years, I felt, *"Now's the time."* I went on to University and then on to Huron College.

As I was going on in those years I had my faith in Christ but I hadn't accepted myself totally — and I hadn't accepted my people either. I was then assigned to my first parish. Where was it? Right back on Walpole Island. I found my ministry right with the alcoholics — the very people I had trouble with. They knocked on the doors at all hours of the day and the rectory was right across from the bootleggers. It couldn't have been closer.

I remember a knock on the door in the middle of the night. A young fellow said, "Can I come in?" I let him in — and he had a gun. He said "Laverne are you ready to die?" I said, "No!" I sat down and he sat up on a step and then he pointed the gun. I was able to pray and just remain calm. I wasn't worried about dying but I thought it would hurt. After a while I went over and took the gun from him and removed the bullets. Then he followed me out to the kitchen. He grabbed a knife from the sink and held it to my throat. Finally, he just started slashing the cupboard.

I didn't see him for a while after that. Another time, he called again. He said he felt like killing someone and asked me to come over. He felt as long as I was present, he could control himself . . . finally after a struggle, he took the bottle of beer he had been drinking and poured it down the drain. I wish I could say that he had a happy ending — but he didn't. He died in a car accident because of alcohol.

But, I look at others and I was able to reach out to them and help them in some way. Another fellow I grew up with always came over and asked for money. I knew he would blow it on booze. I said, ''O.K. — here's the money . . . do what you want. I'll give it to you . . . do what you want — but it's between you and God.'' Another time I lashed out at him, ''Look at what you're doing to yourself. You've lost your dad through alcohol. If there was a choice between a bottle and a woman — you'd take the bottle.'' One night while I was having a Bible study, he called and said, ''I want to quit.'' I left the Bible study and took him into a treatment centre.

The result was he finally made it. He had a car and a nice house. He died a premature death. It was probably related to the way he had lived for so many years. At the funeral, I knew that he had been healed. When I left my parish at Walpole, I could feel really proud — I was no longer ashamed of my own people.

I remember once when our house was broken into — it was the down and outers, the people who were alcoholics who came over and asked how they could help. When I begin to ask, ''Why on the reserve is there so much sickness," I am reminded that there has also been much healing and I can say with the psalmist, "I praise you because I am made in a wonderful way . . . what you have done is wonderful."

I know this very well in my life.

Laverne Jacobs
Oakville/Walpole Island,
Ontario

Prayer for meditation
Lord,
you stretch out your hand to deliver us,
you are beside us as we walk with trouble.

Your steadfast love endures forever.

Prayer for all people
That we may hold firmly to the message of good news, let us pray to the Lord.

SIXTH SUNDAY AFTER EPIPHANY
or between 8 and 14 May

Rejoice and leap for joy, for behold, your reward is great in heaven. *Luke 6.23*

Readings
Jeremiah 17.5–10   *Psalm 1*
1 Corinthians 15.12–20   *Luke 6:17–26*

I try to make my children understand that they have to teach their children what is right. Until they finish school, they have to learn how to live. After they finish school,

they have to make their own way. As they go, they will be meeting many bad habits. When they get to be around thirty or so, they will have many difficulties — then is the time things change. They are either on the bad way — or the right way. They have their own children by then — and they have a big job as parents.

From forty on there is another period when, if they have children, it's their job to teach them the right way.

I can still remember in school, in science study, there was a picture of the earth and you could see it, the many layers of the earth being cut. There are many layers and stages, different levels of earth and soil and rock, and each has its own place. That picture of the earth is how life is. From our fifties to seventies, there is a time of helping others to know how to live their lives. When I look back on my own life I find, too, that I see what I came through. Like the science picture it reflects, too, where the earth was cut. I find also that having the spiritual life has helped me from giving up.

With all the bad things I have met, I couldn't keep on living if it had not been for God, always being there, always willing to take me back as one of his children.

I have been asked to speak at A.A. a few times. They asked me what I thought. I told them that God has created everything. God has put us above the animals and given us the earth to look after; I told them to think of these things, and look after their spirits and their bodies. Always to think that what they have to look after is not theirs, it is God's. Everything is sacred. For that reason, they must look after themselves. They must never break a tree, or damage even a stone. Above all, they must always try to find the talent that God has given them and try to carry it out.

I have had people come back to me later and thank me. I was glad to know that they had grasped what it was that I was trying to say to them about these things.

Jessie Saulteaux
Carry the Kettle,
Saskatchewan

Prayer for meditation
Creator God,
you have created everything and it is good —
the trees, the earth, the animals,
and above all, human life.

We pray that we may protect and care for all of life,
for the earth, for the animals and plants,
and for the treasure which is ours,
in our bodies and in our spirits.

We give thanks for those who show us
what it is to live in the light of your love.

Prayer for all people
That we may fully understand the truth that Christ was raised from the dead so that all may be made alive in Christ, let us pray to the Lord.

SEVENTH SUNDAY AFTER EPIPHANY
or between 15 and 21 May

A new commandment I give to you, that you love one another as I have loved you. *John 13.34*

Readings

Genesis 45.3–11, 15   *Psalm 37.1–12*
1 Corinthians 15.35–38, 42–50   Luke 6.27–38

Elders who work with the Dr. Jessie Saulteaux Resource Centre model gentleness and strength in the face of anger. The Cree word *Keyamawin* means finding an inner peace and waiting for the right moment. This is reflected in the Scripture, "Those who wait for the Lord shall renew their strength."

In the search for a site to house the Dr. Jessie Saulteaux Resource Centre, many locations in Winnipeg were explored. The search began in 1987, and in 1988 the decision was made to lease a vacant school for ten years.

The process of settling into the school began and some renovations were started. In mid-summer, some people living near the school began to complain about the possibility of our being their neighbours. They organized residents and retained lawyers to block our plans. After some aggressive community meetings, the school board was placed under stress. The school board began to show it would bow to public pressure and eventually voted to deny our access to the school.

We knew our position was just, but we could not establish a healing place among people who despised us. The Elders said, "You will find a place and you will know when it is right."

We had arranged for Elders who advise the board of the Dr. Jessie Saulteaux Resource Centre to attend two of the meetings of the school board. Some within our community wanted to stand up and respond in anger. The Elders advised us to explain our program calmly and not to respond in anger. They suggested we not be embroiled in a legal battle.

At a meeting with people of the community, we tried to share in prayer and explain what we wanted to do in the school and community. In their fear, they could not believe us and our prayer only angered them.

Within our own community, we had to deal with forgiveness. We worked at healing through ceremony to assist our own need to move from that place and to find healing — to do what the Elders called us to do, to be responsible and to move forward into a place of healing. We had other discussions and conversations which encouraged our healing. This assisted us in not responding in anger or confrontation.

If we were to respond to anger with anger, we would not have been putting our energy where it was needed. Our energy was to go to healing and to continue our pilgrimage of faith.

The joy is that there were some people from that community who walked with us and who still walk with us. Some marvellous things have happened to us out of that struggle. As I recall those days, as painful as they were, I remember the image of the young people of that community speaking in support of us. We have had ongoing connections with people of the community where the school is located and they have given of themselves and their resources for the development of an Aboriginal Centre.

We have found a home in Beausejour, just east of the City of Winnipeg, and we call it a place of healing.

Stan McKay
Winnipeg/Fisher River,
Manitoba

Prayer for meditation
Creator,
you have taught that we are to love and to forgive.

Grant us grace to follow the truth of your words
to bring your kingdom to earth.

Prayer for all people
That understanding we bear the image of Jesus we may
be life-giving spirits in the world, let us pray to the Lord.

EIGHTH SUNDAY AFTER EPIPHANY
or between 22 and 28 May

Shine as lights in the world, holding fast the word of life.
See Philippians 2.15, 16

Readings
Sirach 27.4–7 or Isaiah 55.10–13   Psalm 92.1–4, 12–15
1 Corinthians 15.51–58   Luke 6.39–49

I talk to my young people sometimes.

They come to me and they say, ''Grandmother, I am
bad.''

''Who says you are bad? Who knows you are bad?
Nobody knows who is bad,'' I tell them. ''You're good.
I'm sure there's something good in you, yet. Use that.''

''Thank you, Grandmother,'' they say.

This is the way I talk to my children, my young people.
Only through love will we bring them back. I talk to my
friends sometimes when they ask me — I don't know if
I'm right or not — but this is how I feel about that. I don't

want to tell them that they're doing wrong, that they're no good — I don't do that.

Whatever you ask the young people to do, if you do it with them, they'll all come and work together well.

But, if you ask them, "Be like this" and, "Do this!" — no, this will not work.

Sarah Simon
Fort McPherson, Northwest Territories/
Old Crow, Yukon

Prayer for meditation
Creator,
the rain and snow
come down from heaven, watering the earth.
So shall your word accomplish its purpose.

May we go out in joy and be led back in peace,
as mountains and hills burst out in song.
May we build our foundation upon the rock of your word,
knowing we are acceptable to you as we are.

We give thanks for the example of transforming love
in the lives of your faithful servants, our Elders.

Prayer for all people
That we may be steadfast, immovable, excelling in the work of the Lord, serving him faithfully, let us pray to the Lord.

THE SEASON OF LENT

Create in me a clean heart, O God,
and put a new and right spirit
within me.
Do not cast me away from your
presence,
and do not take your Holy Spirit
from me.
Restore to me the joy of your
salvation,
and sustain in me a willing spirit.

Psalm 51.10–12

We begin our Lenten time with a story about a life lived in the service of God with an awareness of God's presence in all of life. The story assists us in forming our own ideas of how we move as pilgrims through life.

I was born to a large Native family on my mother's side and my father was Scottish. Sometime around 1909, outside the watchful eye of my little grandmother, my father married my mother. There were eight children in all born in the family.

During my childhood, I was very independent. I think now I must have been a real nuisance at times. From the time I was very young, I never let a thing rest until I had grasped it. I remember many things from when I was very, very young. Our family used to move back and forth to Alaska, and I didn't realise why until I read my father's diary recently. My father was a carpenter and I learned that when there was a large building project taking place, we would move back to Alaska.

By the time my father reached the North, our people were living in a permanent village. A Scotsman by the name of Dan Cadzou had established a trading post at Rampart House. This became the village where Native people would come together keeping up their way of life and culture, fishing, hunting, and trapping. It was a good family life.

In our families, we were always together. The family was never separated. With each season there were many different things to do — and all the family moved and shared in them.

By that time also, there were Native ministers. Although I was very young at the time, I will always remember Amos Njootli. He was the first ordained Native minister in our village. Bishop and Mrs. Stringer would travel through the North once a year, usually in July. He would travel up the river by boat and over the mountains to the Northwest

Territories to visit all the settlements to make sure the ministry was being carried out. One of the first missionaries, Archdeacon McDonald, had translated our language into Old and New Testaments, prayer and hymn books. As a result, Native ministers were able to teach young and old to read our language and all the church services were done in our own language.

John Tizya was a catechist at the time, responsible for the area of Old Crow. He was a hard worker who moved everywhere with the people, hunting, fishing, and trapping. He taught the younger men and women to read in our language. He did this in camps where the lighting was very poor. As a result, he became blind later in life. He was the first Native to build a log cabin in Old Crow which later became the second village, although the Native people used it as a camping place all their lives before log houses were known.

He used a frying pan to call people to worship. He beat quite a few frying pans before Bishop Stringer on one of his visits found out and took that story back to the church group at home. On his next visit, some kind people had the bishop present John with a hand bell which he used for many years.

The families moved together — but at Christmas and Easter and other major holidays, the settlement came together to visit and to celebrate. When we met, we began with the Holy Eucharist and had Communion together; then we went on to the feasts and traditions of our own culture. This went on for a couple of weeks — and then we went back with our families.

The main thing was that we were always together and we were never without our prayer meetings because the ministers always came to us.

When the time came for our education, our father decided to send my older brother and sister to Dawson City. This was thousands of miles from where we were. My mother to this time had been a strong disciplinarian. My father was away a lot of the time — and so discipline was left to my mother. But my father always backed my mother up.

She gave us advice about everything: about the way to live a good life, about going to church. Never a week went by without her lecturing us about something.

When my brother and sister came home for the holiday, they said I should come back with them to Dawson City to school. At this time my father was away in Edmonton. Gas had been found, and he was staking a claim. This took a very long time because it was so far away.

I was excited about going to Dawson City to go to school and so I left with my brother and sister. I never remember getting homesick — although my sister did. I was like that; I would make up my mind to do something and then I would always press forward to do it.

When my father returned from Edmonton the following year and we returned from school, he said "Enough! You have had enough school. You must know how to read and write well enough to get along with the white man — now, you must learn to live in the culture of your mother."

I know how to tan and hunt and trap. I learned by pestering people and asking how to do things. I must have been a terrible nuisance when I was young.

I decided one day I was going to learn to read in my own language. I followed my mother around with a copy of the prayer book in my own language. I learned the Lord's Prayer first. Then, all of a sudden the whole thing opened up to me. I was so amazed.

Sunday was a reading day. In our family on Sundays we all read together. Then we would also visit. In the whole village, no-one worked on Sunday. This was a day when we would visit and give each other tea.

For two or three years, we had no ordained minister and so anyone who could read helped with the services. We had lay readers. When the ordained minister would come, we would have all the weddings and baptisms together. People were all dedicated to the church — everyone from grandmothers to the children and grandchildren.

Today, young people don't go to church. On weekends, they seem to sleep all day and have no time for church. When I see this, I just feel so sad.

When I was married and had my own family, I had to send my children thousands of miles away to get their education. When I sent them to Dawson City, they couldn't go to the public school because they were Indian. Their father was Native — and so the bishop had to hire a private teacher to teach them.

I wanted my children to have an education. I used to try myself to teach them the basics. In the evening, when I was busy at home, I tried to help them.

I understood that the next step if they wanted to go on in school was to go to a residential school. People said that my children would not be allowed to go to a regular high school. I said that I would see about that.

I went to talk to the Indian Agent and I said to him, "My children are ready for high school now and I would like them to go to high school. Are they able to go to the high school?" The Indian Agent said, "I don't see why not," and he turned around in his swivel chair and he called the principal and talked to him. The principal said they could enrol in Whitehorse in the fall.

I then moved with the children to Whitehorse. When they had done their education in Whitehorse and it was time for the older girls to take training, I moved again with them to Vancouver. This is how it was: I followed my family from place to place.

During the time in Whitehorse, I sat on the Regional Indian Advisory Board. I later sat on the National Indian Advisory Board. When I was first elected to the Regional Board, the meetings were held in Vancouver. The National meetings were in Ottawa and so I travelled later to Ottawa for that.

At the time I also had a full-time job working to support my family. Unfortunately, my husband ran into problems with alcohol, and I couldn't deal with that and still raise the children — so I left him and supported my family by working as a cook. I was also very involved with the church at that time. I helped at the church where I could. I was in the A.C.W. and I tried to set an example for my children by working for the church. One Christmas we offered to decorate the church. We sure enjoyed doing it. Always, when the church needed our services, we tried to help.

I sometimes look back and wonder how I did as much as I did. I was lucky during that time that my bosses were understanding and allowed me to take time from my job to do the travelling I needed to do outside of my work. I can say from my own experience that God does help. God's spirit is always with us. If we keep one hand in God's, and have faith, we will find that we can do many things.

It was a busy life and it still is. I have now moved to Vancouver. My daughter asked me to try it for a few months just to see if I liked it — and I liked it so I have stayed.

I've got a vast job now. I have to oversee the lives of my whole family. Our family have many problems. No-one lives their life without problems. We can expect that no matter how hard we work, no matter what we do, we will still have problems. But, I believe we have to deal with our problems within the family. If we can't deal with them within our own family, then we can go outside for the help we might need. But we have first to try to deal with them within our own families with prayer and with understanding.

I look at the world today, and I see so many people on welfare and so many children being neglected. It seems to me that the reason for this is there is not much family life.

It starts with the family. Each family must take responsibility. If each family were to get married in church, and make their promises and then carry their own responsibility to see their children were fed, clothed, and spiritually nourished — and they have to be nourished spiritually — then it would be different. This is the responsibility of the parents. If each family took that responsibility seriously, then, I think half the problems would be solved.

So, I try to follow this way. I know my own family makes many mistakes. I used to emphasize that it is alright to make mistakes. We are only human and we make mistakes. But, if we keep on making the same mistakes, then we are very stupid because we must learn from our mistakes. Mistakes are the greatest teacher we have.

I talk to all my grandchildren. I feel responsible for them. One of my oldest grandchildren was having problems with alcohol. Somehow during this time, he got involved with the Jehovah's Witnesses. I didn't know about this — and heard about it in a round about way. He had said, ''Don't tell granny!'' He felt this way because he was afraid I would object.

When I found out, I said, ''Mark is an adult — and if this helps him in living a good life, in taking care of himself and

69

takes him off alcohol, and makes him happy, then that is good."

These are the kind of things that I have to deal with. If things work out smoothly and satisfactorily, then I just let it go, I can't have any objections.

All of us are responsible for our own lives and our own families. As I have said, the beautiful childhood that I had is almost completely vanished. Now, people are trying to get the old traditions back.

When I went to Sorrento, I had a beautiful spiritual experience which set me on to the second phase of my life. God has plans for your life when you look to God for guidance.

I tried to help the church and Native ministries when I could. They had been meeting in church basements — and wanted to have a nice place. We met a few times and decided to rent a place which was an unused United Church and that is how the Native ministries began. But, it was hard trying to start up a Native ministry. It was hard trying to get a congregation together. Only two or three people came regularly. Many came to weddings and baptisms, but very few came on Sundays.

Even though I was active and had my own place at St. Paul's, I wanted to be helpful to Native ministries because I knew that often Native people feel more comfortable meeting together. I feel that Native people in cities feel scattered. Wherever they live, it's difficult to go places by bus — and some don't have cars. Going to ''all-white'' churches is not comfortable for them either.

I myself feel that way at times if I am in an ''all-white'' gathering. I always try to make things work out. When I first came to Whitehorse, Yukon, people told me, ''Don't go to that Anglican church. People will send you away.'' I went to church and nothing happened.

I have never experienced an embarrassing situation except in Dawson. I was all dressed up and the usher sent me to sit in a certain place. This was fine. The next week, he did the same — and I noticed that all the Native people were sent to sit in the same place. I was really put out. Because the police and other white people I had met in my own community had never treated me in this way, I never expected this — and I was shocked. I also went to the hotel and found that the manager made excuses about why I couldn't stay. I found out that the doctor who was there at the time told them that Native people were sick and had tuberculosis. But, I was not sick — and we didn't have T.B.

This was the only time that I have experienced such things — and it didn't last long because I didn't pay attention to it. All my life, I would never take bunk from anyone. I found that the best thing to do is to nip things in the bud. If someone says something to hurt you, then give it right back. If I do this, then they become my friends.

Once in Vancouver, I sent my boys to register with the Y.M.C.A. They waited there all morning — and when they came home, they said that people behind them in the line had been registered, but they had not been registered. I called the "Y" and asked if they took Native boys. They said they did. I explained what had happened. I spoke to three people before I was through. They said if the boys came down in the afternoon, they would be registered. I said they should have been registered in the morning. And when I told the boys they could go back to register, they didn't want to go anymore and so I didn't send them back.

White people are like other human beings. If you tell them why things are wrong, they often understand. I have a high respect for some people in the white race.

There are some though who are very friendly in gatherings

71

where there are mostly Native people. But, when you meet them in the post office or a place where there aren't many Native people, they will sometimes ignore you completely. I am always ready to greet people — but such a person as this, I ignore, just as they do me. They pretend they do not see me.

It works in many different ways. If you treat people fairly and let them know you know what they are doing, it works best. For myself, I didn't know I was part white until other children called me a half-breed.

This is the journey I have been on thus far: all this I tell about myself in humbleness. Without God's help I would never have come this far. I look back and wonder, ''How did I do it?'' I know it is because I had wonderful parents, one white and one Indian. I learned from both. My father learned the language of my mother — although he didn't speak it as well as we did. Best of all, my parents respected one another.

Clara Tizya
Vancouver, British Columbia/
Old Crow, Yukon

ASH WEDNESDAY

If today you hear his voice, harden not your hearts. *Psalm 95.7–8*

Readings
Joel 2.1–2, 12–17a   *Psalm 103.8–18*
2 Corinthians 5.20b–6.2(3–10)   *Matthew 6.1–6, 16–21*

An important part of my chaplaincy training was learning to prepare written reports on my sessions with patients. These were called verbatims. This, of course, was never done while talking to a patient, but as soon as possible after ending the session. It would be very disturbing to most patients to have notes taken while talking to them.

When preparing a verbatim, one wrote what had been said and analysed it. Later, one could review what had been written and these written verbatims helped in work with a patient.

I remember a man that I used to counsel. He was an out-patient and I saw him once every two to three weeks for several months. He had a problem with alcohol and would become very abusive with his family when he drank. He was then remorseful, and, in his remorse, he came to see me.

This man could pray beautifully. He was able to express himself eloquently with all the right words and expressions. It was pleasant to listen to his voice and the words he said. However, he continued to have the problem with alcohol and with his family.

When I reviewed his verbatims and particularly his prayers, I realized that his problem appeared to be his inability to accept his alcoholism and the responsibility for his actions. He kept asking God to do this thing for him or that thing for him. He could not admit that he had done anything wrong. It was not his fault, it was someone else's actions that had caused him to drink or to be abusive. He could not accept that he had to do something himself, that he had to change, and that he needed God's help to do that. He was denying that he had anything wrong with himself.

This is a common problem with all of us; it is part of being a human being. We find it hard to accept what we are at times. It is only when we come to the realization that with God to help us, we can accept what we are, without condemning ourselves, that we are able to change and to heal ourselves. We then can move to live a more useful and comfortable life.

If I had not used verbatims in my work with this patient, I might have missed out the opportunity to help him because I was so impressed with his gift of speech and expression. It was only after analysing my written verbatims that I was able to help him.

Phyllis Keeper
Winnipeg, Manitoba/
Big Trout Lake, Ontario

Prayer for meditation
Creator God,
as we accept your grace, freely offered,
may we see your salvation.

Help us to turn again to you.

Prayer for all people
That we may be reconciled to God, let us pray to the Lord.

FIRST SUNDAY IN LENT

We shall not live by bread alone, but by every word that proceeds from the mouth of God. *Matthew 4.4*

Readings
Deuteronomy 26.1–11   *Psalm 91.9–16*
Romans 10.8b–13   *Luke 4.1–13*

I was chosen by my family to go out to school to study to be a clergyman with the Anglican church. With two other boys I went with two missionaries and two paddlers in a canoe. Sometimes, when there were rapids, we walked along the bank beside, and when it was more calm, we went into the canoe. We travelled by canoe for one week before we reached the railway and we went by railway the rest of the way.

The community I came from was a Christian one, a Bible-believing community. We had the Bible and a hymn book and a prayer book. We had a copy of *Pilgrim's Progress* which in my language is translated as "The Traveller" and also another called *The Pathway of Life*.

We had some other books by Rev. William Walton, a man who had spent forty years among the Native people in the James Bay area, and he had translated the Ten Commandments and *The Dawn* and a small history of the Anglican Church. These were the only books that people had, and they used them all the time.

My parents went to church and had family devotions as well. People lived in tents and tipis in those days — and in the evening when you went out walking, you could hear all around, the people in their tents and tipis singing and saying their evening prayers. That was how it was when I was a boy.

The missionaries tried to educate us. There was a one-room school house and we used slates. They made an awful racket when you wrote on them. That's the way we started — but some thought they wanted more and that's how I found myself in the canoe — which I didn't want.

But that was what my parents decided should be. I was one of the first ones to go out of the community. It was hard for my parents. No one had gone out before and could tell them how the people who were going to be taking their places as parents would treat their children. And they didn't know if their children would ever come back.

Some of the children who went out got sick, got tuberculosis or something else — and didn't ever come back. There was a small cemetery outside the school with the graves of the children who had died. That's what happened to some.

The good Lord has his hand on me and I found the school quite good.

Redfern Louttit
Moose Factory, Ontario

Prayer for meditation
Creator God,
you are with us in our experiences,
in our temptations.

Your angels guard and protect us.
Your love surrounds us.

We come into your presence knowing
everything is a gift from you.

May we open our eyes to the depth of your love
and seek to follow your ways.

We give thanks for the people whose sacrifices
have been great in attempting to honour your word.

We pray for children everywhere,
separated from families and homes.

We pray for the child in each of us separated from you.
May your love deliver and rescue us.

Prayer for all people
That confessing with our lips and believing in our hearts, we may be brought to true understanding that Jesus is Lord of all, generous to all who call on him, let us pray to the Lord.

SECOND SUNDAY IN LENT

If you hear his voice, harden not your hearts. *Psalm 95.7–8*

Readings
Genesis 5.1–12, 17–18   Psalm 127
Philippians 3.17–4.1   Luke 13.31–35 or Luke 9.28–36

The school I went to was on a railway track and close by the highway. At that time there were always trains going in both directions and sometimes we'd run to the side of the tracks and wave at the engineers and they waved right back at us.

This school provided two teachers for the lower grades, and along with other schools run by Indian Affairs, was called an industrial school. They had cows and horses and the Native children who went to these schools were to learn about farming. We got up early in the morning to milk the cows and feed the horses. There was so much work on the farm, that we only spent two and a half hours a day in school. The rest of the time was on the farm.

When we reached high school age we went to the town high school close by. Our books were provided by Indian Affairs, and we spent all day in school.

When I went into seminary, the Church Missionary Society in England over a period of five years gave me £350 because they were very interested in helping the Indian training program. In those days, in the thirties, a pound was about five dollars and it was a lot of money.

I earned pocket money for myself by working in the summers. One summer, I found myself in Churchill.

Quite a lot of children went to high school, although some of them returned home because they were needed. Some of the boys had a very difficult time — and some of the girls too. They had lost their language and found it difficult to communicate. They didn't learn how to trap and live as their parents, and they found when they went back that they were back in the bush and didn't know their families and couldn't communicate with their parents and were lonesome for the people they had known in school. The closest thing they had learned about living was to be farmers. They knew how to look after the horses, how to hitch them up to a wagon, how to feed them, how to make the hay. They knew how to care for the farm, plant the oats, and harvest.

But — there were no farms, no horses, no cows, no fields, nothing like that up on "The Bay." After school, all those things were just memories, something learned in school. In the meantime, we had lost our languages and had to learn them all over again. My parents didn't know me because I was nine when I left and I was eighteen when they saw me again. I didn't go home again until I was twenty-three. I did become a minister — so that part of the dream was fulfilled.

There were children from many different reserves and in school we spoke different languages so we communicated with each other in English. I later learned the dialect on the West Coast of James Bay when I was there ministering.

When I was twenty-three and just graduated, I was out to

change the world. Well, I soon learned that this is a difficult thing to do. I found instead that I had to change myself. And instead of changing the people, the people had to change me. But, during the years I was in school and training, I met the Lord and gave my life to him — and I found I had a message to give.

I learned how to speak the Cree. I learned to read it and I found I liked speaking it. It is an expressive language and very fine to speak.

I retired after forty-one years — and the time seemed to go so fast! I married a girl from East Maine whose mother was a widow. She had had a difficult life — but she raised her children well. We have raised our own family. Our youngest daughter is working in Quebec on programs for the study of Cree. Our oldest daughter works in Ottawa for the Federal Government and our son has worked in Quebec on housing programs and is now managing an airport. During the time I was ministering in many of the communities, I was also a teacher. Indian Affairs educated me as a teacher. I found it really hard to try to live on the clergy salary, so Indian Affairs had a good salary for the teacher which helped a lot.

Later, I got into the Anglican church's National Council of Native Affairs. I have met many people through this work and I find that I am accepted as I am as a Native person. I think the new clergy are going to be different from me and working in a system that is going to be different from the one that I have worked in. I think we're just coming to the edge of a new Native church working in a different way from the church as it is now and we're going to see Native people running things themselves and there will be more Native control and more cooperation between churches.

Redfern Louttit
Moose Factory, Ontario

Prayer for meditation
Lord God,
you have sent the law and prophets
by which we may know your will.

We have known moments
of protesting and crying in the wilderness.

We give thanks for humility and servanthood,
for laughter and the strength to see ourselves as we are.

We give thanks for those who by faithful living
are a model and source of strength to us.

We give thanks for the restoration of the family —
for homes where your love dwells and grows,
for the blessing of children.

Prayer for all people
That we may stand firm, that our humiliation may be trans-
formed and conformed to the glory of our Lord Jesus
Christ, let us pray to the Lord.

THIRD SUNDAY IN LENT

Repent, says the Lord, for the kingdom of heaven is at
hand. *Matthew 4.17*

Readings
Exodus 3.1–15   *Psalm 103.1–13*
1 Corinthians 10.1–13   *Luke 13.1–9*

I'll never forget how angry my father was. He was so
angry I thought that he was going to cry.

There were twelve children in our family. My father was a

grain farmer. He and my mother also planted a garden so we could have vegetables to eat. There was a milk cow to provide milk and butter and chickens to provide more food. What was sad is that when harvest time came, it was the Indian Agent who took over control of all my parents' earnings from the grain. This was because a permit was needed to sell the grain and the Indian Agent had the authority to issue permits. This is why my father was so angry. He would not fully enjoy the benefits of his labour.

My parents were self-sufficient and hard working. My father was a farmer and a carpenter. He built all our homes. He worked hard for long hours and grew grain. In those days he did all the field work using horses. We had horses, a lot of horses. My mother picked rocks and helped with the harvesting and the stooking. I remember babysitting out in the field, and as a child picking weeds in the garden.

Native people have always been self-sufficient. We were a people of vision, with values and with our own religion. When the buffalo were gone, we were put on reserves after the signing of Treaty Seven. Conditions became worse. People were held down. We were isolated from the rest of society. We had to have a permit to leave the reserve, even to sell wood.

With their livelihood gone, our ancestors believed that everything would be provided for if we had treaties — and so they signed Treaty Seven. Education was to be provided but this was turned over to the churches. My parents were among the first Indian children to reside in a residential school.

I remember my grandparents with whom I spent time. They were so much more gentle. They had the Blackfoot way of doing things — so much more gentle even than my own parents. I don't remember them ever shouting or yelling. They kept repeating not to be lazy — but to work hard.

What I learned in residential school about God is not what I know about God today. Then, I learned about a God of fear — always looking to see what I was doing wrong.

Ten years ago, I came to know God in a different way. I began to learn about what this Kingdom of Heaven really means. It is a place of love — of forgiveness and healing — and we can be a part of bringing about that Kingdom to earth. Part of the reason we have to talk about residential schools is to be sure that no one is ever treated in this way again because it was so painful.

We were taken from our parents and placed in a very cold place. Most of the time we were in a basement. We had to stand on benches just to see outside. When we went out to play, we had to stay in the yard.

When I first went there, coal oil was put on my hair. My hair was cut short. We had to wear drab clothes. The younger boys' hair was shaved completely. In the school with twenty-five boys and twenty-five girls, there were strict morals. We were watched every minute and taught a severe religion day and night.

I have mixed feelings about the school, in part, because at the time we were so poor and at the school we at least had enough to eat. At home, we sometimes didn't. This era was the "dirty thirties."

As a Christian, I now understand the Holy Spirit finds us wherever we are. Today, I am a missionary to my own people — so I understand how the missionaries must have felt, going out and trying to do the work of God. Some tried to help, in spite of the difficulties faced. Some were real Christians but others, out of ignorance, treated us cruelly.

There were some terrible things that happened. One girl who ran away from the school was strapped all the way down her back. The principal just kept on beating and beating her. He wouldn't stop. Later on, all the boys beat him — and he was sent away from there. After that, things were better, so something must have happened to change things. Other people must have known there was something wrong.

There was a loss of culture and tradition. We came out of residential school and we didn't want to be Indian. We were taught Native spirituality was heathen and that the ways of the white people were superior.

We have passed those negative things on to our children. I used the strap on some of my children. To this day they have not forgotten that, but I have tried to undo the damage I have done.

People look at our people and they ask, "Why are people this way?" It is because of this history of cultural genocide and paternalism by government.

Since I became a Christian, I know that there are many good things I was taught as well. I was taught to be a leader. I was one of the first to go out to Pincher Creek High School. I was taught to keep going in spite of obstacles. People who went to residential schools are now the backbone of our communities. I have learned to keep on trying — even when it's hard. I was taught about discipline — and I sometimes wish I had taught my own children that.

I understand that the people who were cruel did it out of ignorance. I understand what a wonderful thing it is to know about forgiveness.

I have friends everywhere. It doesn't matter what race people are — what matters most to me is that we are sisters and brothers in Christ. I worked on the Band Councils for eighteen years and during that time, I learned many things and travelled many places. I was involved on a national political level.

Now, I am waiting on God to see where I may be called next. It seems right that I am now serving my own people as a leader in the Church. My bishop has called me to the church I grew up in. Where it is situated is very beautiful, looking out over the Old Man River valley. In the summer it is a wonderful picture. Looking out from the altar of the church you can see all over the valley, green and beautiful — filled with trees and flowers.

I am glad that the Church is listening, that it is open minded so that we may communicate. I have had much training and study towards healing and wholeness — and I and many others desire more than anything else to work at moving beyond the pain to wholeness.

Margaret Waterchief
Lay Pastor at Brochet/
Peigan Reserve, Alberta

Prayer for meditation
Creator,
your servant Moses led his people
into freedom, into new life.

You come to us as you came to prophets of old.
May we be open, prepared to meet you,
to walk with you.

May we find in your surrounding grace
the way to work at bringing your Kingdom on earth.

We give thanks for those who share their experiences
that we might face wrongdoing and stop cruelty.

May we have the courage to see ourselves
as we are, to make things right.
We give thanks for forgiveness and reconciliation.

May we grow together in wisdom and truth,
in the light of your steadfast love.

Prayer for all people
That relying on the rock of Christ, we may be nourished to bring new life, hope, and recovery to our communities, let us pray to the Lord.

FOURTH SUNDAY IN LENT

I will arise and go to my father, and I will say to him: Father I have sinned against heaven and before you.
Luke 15.18

Readings
Joshua 5.9–12   *Psalm 34.1–8*
2 Corinthians 5.16–21   *Luke 15.1–3, 11–32*

At a certain time in my life, I decided I should start to make things right with my father. I told him how sorry I was for the rebellion and the anger in my life.

He never said a thing to me. I was driving the car and he was sitting beside me. I didn't know what to think because he just sat beside me and never said a thing.

Three days later, he began telling me stories, starting with the one about his friend Charlie. He told me that he hated residential school.

When he was sixteen, he and a friend ran away from the school. Home was the first place they would be looked for — so, the two of them ran away to join the army. When they went to the recruiting office, there was no objection to their joining. It was the First World War. They needed anybody they could get.

85

The military decided to separate him and his friend and put them in different units because if they were in the same unit and something happened to one, it would be hard for the other to handle it.

My father found another friend anyway. His name was Charlie, and he was an Indian from northern Manitoba.

Soldiers took turns on lookout. When Charlie was on lookout in the trenches, they were talking together. His friend was standing right beside him — and all of a sudden, he didn't answer. My father tugged his arm. "Charlie," he said, "what's the matter?" But Charlie didn't answer. And all of a sudden my father could see that Charlie had a bullet through his head. He was gone.

Seventeen years old, he was. A stray bullet got him. My father never talked about that for years. He started to cry when he was telling this to me. I imagine he never talked about it before. He must have kept all that pent up inside all those years. Imagine what it must have been like — having that happen at seventeen?

From then on he shared his life more and more. This is how it is in my community; when you show you are ready to listen, you are trusted with the stories. I've heard many stories since then — and they are powerful teachings, wonderful stories to help us to know how to live.

My father also told me my Indian name. Most Cree people have two names — an English name and an Indian name. We often don't tell people of our Indian names — but I tell my children to be proud of their names. Their names are a very important part of their identity.

Art Anderson
Regina/Kāneonuskatēw,
Saskatchewan

Prayer for meditation
Creator God,

Your love guides us toward a new future,
a future where relationships are reconciled,
enriching us and giving us new life,
new life that in turn may enrich our children.

Like the Israelites giving up their manna, desert food,
we find new food — richer and more satisfying.

We give thanks for moments of turning again to your love,
for the love of a parent for a child,
for the opportunity to turn again home,
and the delight of finding your outstretched arms
waiting to embrace us.

Prayer for all people
That we may be reconciled to God, so that in him we
might carry the message of reconciliation as ambassadors
for Christ, let us pray to the Lord.

FIFTH SUNDAY IN LENT

All I care for is to know Christ and the power of his resurrection. *See Philippians 3.10*

Readings
Isaiah 43.16–21   Psalm 126
Philippians 3.8–14   John 12.1–8

I remember the time that it came to me what the death
and resurrection of Jesus meant in my life.

I was a supervisor of school children at the time. As I was

working, I felt a presence approaching me and it seemed a very evil presence. I was feeling very nervous, very uncomfortable. This presence came three times, on three separate days — and I never knew when it would happen. Each time it came only so close, then it went away. I was agitated and upset.

I tried prayer — everything, but nothing seemed to help. Then my brother said that there was a Native Traditional person coming to the reserve to do a ceremony. My brother invited me to come along.

Our reserve still preserves some parts of the Traditional. I have a great respect for the Elders and I knew a little about the Traditional ways and so I said I would come. I brought gifts — a cloth print and some tobacco. By this, the Elder knew that I had something to ask of him.

I explained to the Elder what had happened to me, the fear of the presence that I had felt approaching me. At the ceremony, there was a sacrifice. The Elder talked to me and gave me meat.

As I held the meat in my hand, the sacrifice which had been made in the ceremony, what flashed through my mind was, "This is my body given for you." Suddenly, the idea of how Jesus had died for me became clear. He died as a substitute for us. He laid down his life that we might have life. It was real life, a living thing which was offered when he died. I had always known this, but in that moment, with the meat of the animal in my hand which the Elder had offered to me, I understood — I suddenly understood the full meaning of Christ's offering himself as a sacrifice for me.

As I took that meat, I felt warm inside — it was like a glow. I knew then that the reason that the presence could come only so far was because I am surrounded and protected by Christ, by his love for me.

There are some who would say that it was Native Spiritual Tradition which healed me. Others would condemn me for being involved in a Native ceremony. But, I know that it was the presence of Christ who came to me through my own tradition, through the Elder. It is Christ alone who came to me in that moment in a much deeper way. But it was a way that I understood from my own Native Tradition.

This was a turning point in my life. It was new life for me — and I began to live in the power of his resurrection. I know that was the beginning of my decision to become a priest in the Anglican church. I am a priest in my own community now. I have a lot of respect for the Traditional Elders in the community and they respect me. We work together for good in the community.

I think of Christ and how he came to the people of Israel. At the transfiguration, Christ was walking with Moses and Elijah. The law was brought to earth through Moses — and the prophecies through Elijah. But those were not enough. Christ was the completion of their tradition — and Christ is the completion for us in our time.

This was not to say that our own Tradition was wrong. We have to respect it because that is who we are. Christ comes to us through our own understandings. It should not surprise us that he would come to us through our own Elders; they are men of God doing their best to be instruments of God as they understand God — and they are godly men who understand our own Native ways.

James Isbister
Sandy Lake/Ahtahkakoop Reserve,
Saskatchewan

Prayer for meditation
Creator,
you meet us where we are,
and bring us home.

We come to you with dancing,
with joy and thanksgiving.

We who have gone out weeping —
come home with shouts of joy.

Like Mary, we long to serve you,
to bring your love to others.

Prayer for all people
That we may press on toward the goal of the heavenly call
of God in Christ, let us pray to the Lord.

HOLY WEEK

A perpetual fire shall be kept burning on the altar; it shall
not go out. *Leviticus 6.13*

The 1990 meeting of the All Native Circle Conference
opened with the lighting of the Sacred Fire. The Fire was
located outside a tent where 200 Native United Church
leaders from across Canada were gathering. The Conference carries to each meeting ashes from Sacred Fires of
previous meetings.

Alf Dumont, speaker of the All Native Circle Conference, in
lighting the Fire stated, ''the ashes from the previous fire
are placed with the ashes of this and when you go on, you
are to take the ashes with you as a reminder of the decisions that were made here. Carry them with you remem-
bering that we carry our history with us wherever we go.''

A procession of Elders gathered around the Fire to the sound of a drum, the heartbeat of Mother Earth. Memories of years past drifted over the distant lake, above grassy grounds, rising to meet clouds with the clapping of thunder. As the sounds of the drums rose around the gathering, one could sense the spirit rising above the long-reaching clouds, above misting roads where aspen and pine stood with outstretched arms.

Selections for Easter week include stories which may be incorporated into Passion Sunday, Maundy Thursday, Good Friday, Easter Saturday, and Easter Sunday. Storytellers bring teachings of their traditions joined with experience of the passion and resurrection of Christ in their own lives to bring us new understanding of and insight into the Easter story.

THE SUNDAY OF THE PASSION

Christ became obedient unto death, even death on a cross. Therefore God has highly exalted him and bestowed on him the name which is above every name. *Philippians 2.8–9*

Readings
Isaiah 50.4–9a   *Psalm 31.9–16*
Philippians 2.5–11   *Luke 22.14–23 or Luke 23.1–49*

The first name of my grandmother in the Assiniboine language is Och-Pay-Ota which is translated into English as "Stabbed many times." Her last name has the meaning "Good elk."

Here is how she received her name: when she was fourteen she had a dream. She dreamed that she was attacked and stabbed. In her dream she was told what must be done to bring healing to her wounds. She told this dream to her people.

One day, when she was close to the camp with the women gathering firewood, and the men were out guarding the camp some distance away, she was attacked. Blackfoot tribes often came and tried to take women away to be their wives.

My grandmother fought. She ran up the side of the hill and when she was running she threw snow back to try to slow the man following her and cause him to fall. This made the man very angry, and when he caught her, in his rage, he stabbed her again and again. He stabbed her thirteen times. He did not try to take her. She was found unconscious by her people and taken to a tent where the medicine people administered the healing in the way she herself had seen in her dream. And so it was that in her dream she had prepared them to know how to treat her wounds. She was so badly stabbed that her lungs protruded from her body. I saw her scars from the wounds when I was little, and I felt them on her body.

My grandmother knew about medicines. She said that in all things there was good and bad; she told us about the good — but she never told us about the bad.

There were medicines for earaches and toothaches and for pains anywhere. There were medicines for birth control and for miscarriages and there were only certain people in each community who knew about the medicines; many people used to go to her for the medicines.

Jessie Saulteaux
Carry the Kettle,
Saskatchewan

Prayer for meditation

Creator,
the greatest of your prophets
knew the agony of insult and attack.

Your Son came,
walked with the lonely, the sick, the weak.
He knew pursuit, attack, and suffering.

He came as a servant to bring healing and hope.
He is with a young girl — alone, pursued, and left for
dead.

We give thanks for the gifts within ourselves
which are given to bring healing to ourselves and our
communities — for dreams and for medicines.

Give us the grace to face our own suffering,
to be self-giving and obedient to your will for us.

Lord, let your face shine upon us, your servants.

Prayer for all people

That we may have the mind of Christ who emptied himself
and became a servant, let us pray to the Lord.

MAUNDY THURSDAY

A new commandment I give to you, that you love one
another as I have loved you. *John 13:34*

Readings

Jeremiah 31.31–34   *Psalm 116.10–17*
Hebrews 10.16–25   *Luke 22.7–20*

In our Tradition, we have celebrations to mark the coming

95

of each season. We have celebrations to mark the spring, the summer, the fall, and the midwinter.

In the spring, we have a celebration to be thankful for having survived to the end of the long winter. We give thanks for the return of the ducks and the other birds. Summertime, during the season of berries, towards the end of July, we have a berry feast. We invite whoever wishes to come. We give thanks for the abundance of berries.

In the fall, when the geese leave, we give thanks for their being here. We usually use beaver at this feast time. We ask for guidance at this hard time of the season because we want to survive the winter.

In the middle of January, we have our mid-winter feast, giving thanks for surviving to that time — and praying for continued guidance to the end of the most difficult season.

At these ceremonies, whoever wishes to come is invited to come. We have our ceremony on the floor to remind us always to remain close to the earth. We place food on a tablecloth on the floor — and the people gather around the food. Also placed on the tablecloth is the Sacred Pipe. We do not have sweetgrass as other areas do. Where we live, we use the Sacred Pipe for purification at these feast times.

The chief is the head of each of these feasts. Any who have Pipes may bring the Pipe to share with others at the feast. When the prayers are said, and before the taking of food, the Pipe is passed and each in turn takes a puff of the Pipe.

In addition to the four major feasts to mark the seasons, there is a ceremony for medicines in the fall. We make our own medicines. Each year, we give thanks for the medicines and pray for protection during the year.

We usually have the medicine ceremony at the house of the chief. Each of us brings our own medicines. We make our medicines from the roots and grasses of the earth. Each person takes a bit of whatever medicine he/she has made — and we place these all together. Then we boil and drink the medicine water around the circle.

After everyone in the gathering has had a drink, we take the pipes and give thanks. Whoever wants to take a certain kind of medicine, brings a container in which he takes home some of the medicine. This is to bring the medicine to anyone in his household who may want to take it.

Sanadius Fiddler
Sandy Lake, Ontario

Prayer for meditation
Creator God,
you have put your law within us.
You have made us a people of the new covenant
and have written it upon our hearts.

We give thanks for the fruit of the earth,
for healing oils given to the early church —
by which people were anointed and healed —
blessed each Maundy Thursday.

---

* Notes on Maundy Thursday:
Within the Anglican tradition, Maundy Thursday is a time set aside for important teachings about the role of servant. The Book of Alternative Services includes a liturgy for a ceremony for the washing of feet. This is the day Christ washed the feet of the disciples and so gave to them a glimpse of the role of servanthood.

Maundy Thursday commemorates the Last Supper and the institution of the Eucharist or Communion.

Maundy Thursday within the Anglican tradition is also a time of the blessing of oils which are then kept to be used for prayer and healing throughout all seasons of the year.

We give thanks for the medicines of healing
given to Ojibwa people, blessed at the medicine ceremony.

We give thanks for the knowledge of our ancestors.
May we seek to serve each other in your most perfect will
as you showed in the washing of the feet of your disciples
at the time of the Last Supper.

Prayer for all people
That we may encourage each other to love and to do good
deeds, let us pray to the Lord.

GOOD FRIDAY

Christ became obedient unto death, even death on a cross.
Therefore God has highly exalted him and bestowed on
him the name which is above every name.
Philippians 2.8–9

Readings
Isaiah 52.13–53.12   Psalm 22.1–17
Hebrews 4:14–16; 5.7–9   John 18.1–19.42
                            or John 19.17–30

My grandson was in the hospital, badly hurt in a car
accident. He was transferred from our hospital to Sick
Children's in Toronto. It is a long two-and-a-half-hour drive
to Toronto.

I wanted to go to see him. ''It'll be too hard on you,
Mom,'' my daughter said. None of my family would take
me to see him.

Every day for three weeks I prayed looking out my window
over the lake.

One of my grandsons came over one evening and said, "Someone has a relative in the hospital in Toronto — the same hospital as Bud's in. He came to talk to me. He wants to know — do you want to go with him to Toronto?"

I was so happy. I didn't tell anyone — I just got ready to go. The next day I waited and waited but he didn't come to call for me. I called his house and asked if they had already left. "No, it's tomorrow we're going." I got ready again the next day.

When I walked into the hospital, a nurse came up to me and said, "Are you Gladys Taylor?" I said, "Yes." She said, "Your daughter has called ahead. She's afraid it'll be too hard on you to see your grandson."

The nurse talked to the doctor. They let me go in to see him with the nurse beside me.

When I went into the room, he was naked from the waist up. He had a fever; they were trying to bring it down with a fan. He had just turned sixteen years old, and into his manhood — he was strong. But then, he looked just like a little bird, so frail, propped up, covered with a thin sheet, his head all bandaged up — they'd done operations to try to help him.

I sat close beside him and held his hand in mine. I said to him in Ojibwa, "Bud — can you hear me?" I didn't think that he could hear or understand anything. He was in something like a coma. There was a lot of brain damage. He was unconscious since the accident. I prayed in Ojibwa for him. I talked to him as I talked to him when he was a little boy playing in my house by the lake. Oh — I felt so terrible and I prayed with all my heart."

"Bud, if you can hear me, give me a little sign." I put my hand under his hand. "If you can hear me, give me a little sign that you can hear me, Bud'' — and I felt the faintest touch on my hand where he pressed my palm.

"What are you doing?" the nurse demanded. She asked this as though I were annoying her. I didn't understand why she'd say that. I think she knew I was praying.

"I have come to give my grandson back to the Creator," I said. I couldn't reach him anywhere to kiss him, so I kissed my hand and just rubbed it on his arm. My heart was so touched by his poor, broken life. I prayed:

God in Heaven, help him in his strife.
Forgive him, dear Master,
and carry him home
for all through his life, he's been so alone.

Thank you, Lord Jesus, for hearing my prayer.
I can tell by his peaceful face
that he knows you are there.

O Lord of great pity, the victory is won.
I thank you Lord Jesus, His struggle is done.

Please Heaven deliver my message to my Buddy dear.

The next afternon the phone rang. When I answered, a voice said, "Are you Bud's grandmother?"

I said, "Yes."

"This is the doctor. I am calling to let you know, grandmother, that your prayer is answered; your grandson went home this morning."

Then I knew that my prayer had been answered as I felt a great peace flow over my heart and soul.

Gladys Taylor
Curve Lake, Ontario

Prayer for meditation
Creator,
you are with us always.

We give thanks for those who walk bravely
into dark places thinking not of themselves,
but honouring commitments.

Lord, may we be obedient to your will.

Prayer for all people
That we may approach the throne of grace boldly so that
we may receive mercy and find grace to help in time of
need, let us pray to the Lord.

THE SEASON OF EASTER

*Christ our Passover has been
sacrificed for us; therefore let us
keep the feast.*

1 Corinthians 5.7–8

THE GREAT VIGIL OF EASTER

Rejoice, heavenly powers! Sing, choirs of angels! Exult, all creation around God's throne! Jesus Christ, our King, is risen!

Readings
Exodus 14.10–15.1   Psalm 114
Romans 6.3–11   Luke 23.55–24.9

When we have bitterness instead of love in our hearts, we may sometimes find ourselves able to minister to people who also have bitterness in their hearts. But, we will drive all others away.

We have to make a start somewhere to undo the many feelings of hurt that we have. If we do not deal with the hurt, it is like a thorn under our skin. It seems to get worse and worse until it festers and then forms a callous, the hurt is so bad.

Every time you think about it, it gets worse until finally the only way to heal it is by getting something sharp to lift off the callous. When the callous is off, just a little pressure, a little squeeze will bring it out.

We have to let go of our old feelings. We will feel the callous has been lifted as we embrace. Instead of feeling the bitterness, we feel the flowing of love as we embrace the ones that we had been thinking about in bitterness.

This is what it means to lift the callous so that it lessens the pain: we must embrace the ones we thought were the cause of all our suffering. Life isn't so long that we can waste our time walking backwards.

Gladys Taylor
Curve Lake, Ontario

104

Prayer for meditation
Creator,
the mountains skipped and the earth trembled
when you brought the tribes of Israel into freedom.
You sent your Son to die for us that we might have new
life.

May we grasp the freedom you offer with outstretched
arms.

Prayer for all people
That we may be united with Christ in a resurrection like his
so that we might no longer be enslaved to sin, let us pray
to the Lord.

EASTER — DURING THE DAY

Christ our Passover has been sacrificed for us; therefore let
us keep the feast. *1 Corinthians 5.7–8*

Readings
Acts 10.34–43 or
* Isaiah 65.17–25*
1 Corinthians 15.19–26 or
* Acts 10.34–43*

Psalm 118.14–24
John 20.1–18 or
* Luke 24.1–9*

Where I come from, people from the South would say it is
very barren — but we who live there know that it is filled
with life.

Many people in the North are carvers. People in the South
recognize the beauty of the carvings. A soapstone carving
has its own life. Each carving carries the vision of the
carver.

If you were to see the stone before the carver touched it

105

and gave it the life that it has, you would not be impressed. It is only a rough piece of stone, a chunk of unshaped rock. It is the carver who gives it the life that it has.

Faith in Christ is like that. I have come to faith in Christ and I believe that when you have faith in Christ, you are shaped by Christ to become what you really are inside yourself — just as the rock is shaped by the vision of the carver. The carver sees beyond the rough outer rock to the possibilities of the beauty of the carving. He has a vision of the rock and he shapes it to be what he sees within the rock and so he makes a beautiful carving.

When this carving is presented, everyone knows and understands that the carving is beautiful. Each carving is different from the next. Each has a life of its own and is a work of art.

If you look at a group of carvings, you may tell from the style which are by one stone carver, and which by another. Each carver has a personal style — and if you know the style, then you will know the carver. But, each carving is still different, even by the same carver.

This is how it is with life in Christ. Each person becomes more what he/she really is in one's own culture — not less. This is what I see in the life of Christ. You do not become like someone else. You do not try to set aside the things you have learned in your own life, your language, your understandings of life in order to take on something that is really someone else's. You become more what you are in your own culture — with your own teachings.

Everyone understands carvings to be very beautiful and very valuable. The beauty is obvious to all regardless of their culture. People might never have seen the North where these carvings are made. They might not understand

107

how to us it is filled with life when it appears to be barren. Yet, they understand and recognize the beautiful art.

So it is with life in Christ. Christ is the fulfilment of our own culture and our own language and our own understandings. Each culture has its own beauty. When we are in Christ, and we follow Christ, there is a beauty in the image of who we are just as there is a beauty in the carvings which are carved with the vision of the carver.

Andrew Atagotaluk
Pond Inlet, Northwest Territories

Prayer for meditation
Creator, great Carver,
you hold us in your hands
and see the inner parts of our being.

Your Son, Christ, has been raised from the dead,
and has destroyed death.

May we, your children, heirs of your new covenant,
live out the resurrection promise in our lives.

You who are our strength and our salvation,
open to us the gates of righteousness that we may enter.

Prayer for all people
That we may understand the message of peace brought by Christ, and preach and testify that everyone who believes in Christ receives forgiveness through his name, let us pray to the Lord.

SECOND SUNDAY OF EASTER

Have you believed, Thomas, because you have seen me?
Blessed are those who have not seen and yet believe.
John 20.29

Readings

Acts 5. 27–32   Psalm 2
Revelation 1.4–8   John 20.19–31

I was chosen by my family when I was nine years old to be a servant of God, a priest. When I was nine, I went in a canoe with two priests and two paddlers.

I was so far from my home that I never went home until I was eighteen. When I stepped out of the canoe, my parents looked up and said, "Who's that handsome young clergyman?" They didn't recognize me. I couldn't talk to them because they spoke no English, and I had lost my language.

The teenage years were especially hard. There was a person at the school who was like a foster mother — and she was good to us. But, it wasn't the same as if you had a real father and mother to guide you through the struggles.

My parents had a bit of status in the community because they had a son who went out in this way to be a clergy-man — but it was also hard. Although my parents were admired, many of the other people in the community admitted they could not have done the same themselves, to send out a child so young to go to school.

I think it was hardest on my mother. After I left, my father said it was a long time before my mother had her heart in her work. There were others at home, but they say it was very hard on her when I left.

When I was a freshman in university taking theological studies, everybody knew I was an Indian. They had certain ideas of how Indians would be.

At initiation days in the college, because I was Indian, they had me do an Indian War Dance in the streets of Toronto.

109

They must have given this a lot of thought. They had feathers fastened to a cardboard piece and they fastened it to my head. I stomped around on Bloor Street whooping it up as I thought a war dance would be — although I never saw a war dance in my life. Where I came from, people were Bible-believing Christians. I didn't know what a war dance was!

Well, I must have looked funny.

Since I was an Indian, they thought I must know how to run so they asked me to be on the five-mile running team. I didn't know how to run! I'd never tried to run in my life — but I didn't want to disappoint them, so I said I would. Maybe there was something to it because I trained and learned how to run. Every year that I was there, we won the first prize.

I have a band number. I somehow found it hard, being a number. It was as though I didn't have a name. When I graduated and was a young clergyman, people in the communities I served thought I knew everything — even what the weather would be like the next day. For some reason they thought of someone educated as having all knowledge.

I have had a good life and many opportunities to serve the Lord for over fifty years. My time of serving is over. There are different ways to do things now and a whole new generation of young leaders. They will do things in a different way — and this is good.

In choosing new leaders, I remember the apostles and the difficulty they had in choosing leaders. We have to be careful in the choosing of leaders for our community — but I believe in the Bible and I go by the words:

"Be not afraid; only believe!"

Redfern Louttit
Moose Factory, Ontario

110

Prayer for meditation

Creator,
you are Alpha and Omega,
beginning and end.

May we be wise, serving you with fear
taking refuge under your wings.

Lord, come —
stand among us and show us your peace.
We long to be believers; help us in our unbelief.

We give thanks for the leaders who have gone before us.
May we, living in the knowledge of your resurrection,
consider in our hearts how we might serve you.

Prayer for all people

That we may be obedient to God rather than any human
authority, let us pray to the Lord.

THIRD SUNDAY OF EASTER

Lord Jesus, open to us the scriptures; make our hearts
burn within us while you speak. *See Luke 24.32*

Readings

Acts 9.1–20   Psalm 30.4–12
Revelation 5.11–14   John 21.1–19 or John 21.15–19

When I took chaplaincy training I went to classes, attended
conferences and workshops and also did Bible studies. An
important part of our training was visiting patients in hospital wards. I usually spent mornings in classes and after-
noons in the wards. I had many interesting experiences
during that time.

In one ward, a woman was brought in from up North. She was about fifty-three years old and could understand only very simple words in English. Her first language was Saulteaux. When she realized I could speak her language, she was really happy and asked me to visit her whenever I had time.

I·really got attached to her. I visited with her every chance I had. She asked me what my job was in the hospital. She didn't understand the word chaplain. I don't think there is a word to say chaplain in my language. I wasn't ordained so I couldn't say I was a minister. I told her I was training to learn how to work with people in the hospital and to pray with them if a patient or family requested. She was so happy to find someone to pray with her.

She started telling me about herself. She was in a very weak condition. She had lost a lot of weight. She told me that her daughter-in-law had died with cancer and left three little children. They were three, four, and seven years old. Her son and daughter-in-law were very, very, young when they got married. It was two years since the daughter-in-law died and she had cared for the children since, because her son couldn't cope with them.

You could tell how much she loved those kids. She would say, "I hope they're taking care of them good. The three of them need a lot of hugging. I hope they have enough to eat."

One of the interpreters had interpreted for her that morning. She understood that she had to have a very serious operation. She started talking about her grandchildren. She said, "I wouldn't worry so much if I didn't have those three little kids."

She had to stay in hospital for a while before her operation because she had to build up her strength. She was quite

112

weak when she arrived in hospital. When she went into the operation, she was still unconscious two days later. I went to see her doctor to have him tell me about her. He knew I was always there for her when I had time. He told me, "She is very, very sick. She waited too long to see a doctor — and has been suffering quite a while. If she had come in as soon as she knew there was trouble, it would have been better."

I explained to him that you can't always do this on a reserve. On a reserve, you might know that something was wrong and if there was a nurse, they might give you something. Sometimes you might not even be able to see a nurse. There are usually no doctors available.

The third day after her operation, I had to leave. As part of my training, I had to write a paper about Genesis, do a presentation, and attend a conference. I didn't want to leave her. I talked to one of the supervisors of my training and was told I would fail in this part of the training if I didn't attend the conference. I was worried about her. I kept on praying with her when she was unconscious. I remember the last time I went up to see her, I really prayed and held her hand as I prayed. She never moved.

As I prayed, I told her, "I have to leave. I have to go because of my training. I will be back in ten days." I prayed to God that her grandchildren needed her so bad here on earth, but whatever is God's will. I felt as though she was my own sister. I wished always to treat the patients as my own family. I thought of how I would feel if the patient was my own sister, my own daughter, or my own mother.

I prayed, "Whatever happens, God take care of it." I prayed that the children would be in a home where they would be loved if something happened to their grand-mother.

I knew that I didn't have the power to do any of these things. I had to put my trust in God. When I went into the conference, there was a chapel there. I prayed there. My prayers showed me that I was trying to do things myself. I was trying to be there for her — instead of letting God be there for her.

Sometimes we are in God's way when we can't let go. I felt so much better when I felt that I could let go and let God work with her.

When I came back ten days later, I was still sometimes not believing. Sometimes we lose the feeling that God is going to take care of things.

I avoided going to see her when I came back. I went first to the wards I was assigned to. The last ward I went to was her ward. We were very busy, and when I came back, I didn't trust enough. I was kind of afraid to visit her. I was afraid I would find out that she was gone. I thought the nurse might come and say she had died. That's why I went to visit her last.

When I went into her ward, she was sitting there swinging her legs over the side of the bed and eating lunch. And she said to me, ''Oh, Phyllis, I'm so glad to see you back. I thought they might send me home before you came back. You know, I knew that you'd been praying for me.''

I told her about how I felt, how I was so scared. God shows us how many things he can do — and yet we still don't believe. We were hugging and crying together. When I saw her before I went away, she had many machines attached to her body. When I came back, she was only on intravenous. She was doing well and told me she was going to be going home that week sometime.

She said, ''Let's give thanks to God. See, I can eat my meals too.'' She took her bread and wanted to give me

114

half. I told her, "No, I won't have half because that is all you have — and you need it to build up your strength. But, I will take a small piece and we will share it like the Eucharist and give thanks to God."

If I had been able to give Eucharist like an ordained priest, I would have — but I couldn't. So, I took a cup of water from the sink in the ward and we had Eucharist with water and bread.

I learned from this that I have to let go and let God and not be in his way.

Phyllis Keeper
Winnipeg, Manitoba/
Big Trout Lake, Ontario

Prayer for meditation
Creator God,
like the psalmists of old, brought from death,
like Paul, blinded on the road to Damascus,
deliver us, teach us your ways.

Worthy is the Lamb.
May we understand your will and your ways.

May we love and serve your people
as you would have us love and serve in your name.

Prayer for all people
That encountering the risen Lord, we may bear witness to his love and live out the good news in our own lives, let us pray to the Lord.

FOURTH SUNDAY OF EASTER

I am the good shepherd, says the Lord: I know my own and my own know me. *John 10.14*

Readings
Acts 13.15–16, 26–33   *Psalm 23*
Revelation 7.9–17   *John 10.22–30*

I have walked long on this earth and have had a very long life.

I have seen that the way to follow God is to do something for good; we must share with others.

This is how we see God: these teachings are from God and I know God is in this. God's presence is in the teachings.

I know also that the power of evil is real.

In our own family, I was taught to listen. I try to talk to my sons; they believe they are wiser than I.

This is a struggle for me: we need not accumulate things — but we are to share.

The central thing, the thing that leads to eternal life, is love; and the power of living is in love.

The legal systems of the earth are not the laws of God. If we think the legal systems of the earth are difficult — think about the laws of God which are even more difficult.

Think of me as a friend. I have no enemies: remember me in friendship.

Benjamin Wood
Nelson House, Manitoba

Prayer for meditation
Creator God,
you are our shepherd,
the Lamb at the centre of the throne.

You call all nations to kneel at your throne.
May we be guided to springs of the water of life;
may we understand the love you proclaim.

Prayer for all people
That we may understand the message of salvation sent to
prophets of old has been fulfilled for us in the resurrection
of Christ, let us pray to the Lord.

FIFTH SUNDAY OF EASTER

A new commandment I give to you, that you love one
another as I have loved you. *John 13.34*

Readings
Acts 14.8–18   *Psalm 145.14–22*
Revelation 21.1–6   *John 13.31–35*

The gospel of Luke tells us how Jesus came into the
world, shared the good news and trained his followers.
Luke was someone who knew Christ really well. The
gospel tells us this.

In the early life in the church, all were together; they were
operating as a community. They were working together
and it wasn't one do this — another do that — it was all
together sharing burdens, sharing the yoke.

When I first became involved in the training of Native
clergy, I was conscious that there was in the usual Western culture and version of Christianity, a sense of the
Creator being so radically different from the creation as to
be almost indifferent to it. This was different from the
understanding of creation within the Native clergy.

When I was visiting the clergy school, an Elder and I went

117

down to the shore after the service. There was a beaver swimming out in the water. The Elder called to the beaver. The beaver stopped in the middle of the bay, swam straight up to the shore — and then walked up the shoreline and came right to where we were standing.

For me, it was quite astonishing. For the Native person, this was not unusual — because his understanding of creation includes the whole of creation much more than our own Western way.

Michael Peers
Toronto

Prayer for meditation
Creator God,
you satisfy the desire of every living thing;
you watch over all who love you,
all creatures of the earth bless your name.

You make all things new,
dwelling among us as our God.
May we love each other as you have loved us.

Prayer for all people
That we may turn to the living God who made the heaven and the earth and the sea and all that is in them, let us pray to the Lord.

SIXTH SUNDAY OF EASTER

If you love me, you will keep my word, and my Father will love you, and we will come to you. *See John 14.23*

Readings
Acts 15.1–2, 22–29   Psalm 67
Revelation 21.10, 22–27   John 14.23–29

I am a priest on my own reserve. I am familiar with the understandings of the Native Spiritual Tradition, and I could tell people about many of those understandings — yet I am Christian also. I think it is important to talk about the different approaches and to respect the different understandings. Here is an example of what I mean.

In my community, there was a death — and the people called and asked if I could do the funeral. I said that I would. Later, a young man called and said that I would not be needed after all because the family had decided that they would like to have a Traditional funeral. This was on the same day as the funeral and only a few hours before I was to go.

A while later, I received another call. This time the young man was in great distress. The funeral had not gone on. The quarrel between those who wished a Traditional funeral and those who wished an Anglican funeral had split the family in half — and the funeral could not go on.

He was very apologetic again. I said that I would be happy to come. I went to them and did the funeral for them. The young man had wanted to push the Native Traditional ways — but there were many in the family who had not known the Traditional way and who were very distressed by the Traditional.

A funeral, a death, is so difficult and it was hard for the family to have such a quarrel just then. This young man meant well, but he was wrong.

There was a discussion and Traditional Elders solved the problem. Although they themselves were most comfortable with the Traditional way, they knew the Anglican service was familiar to this family — and was what the family really wanted. They explained this in such a way to the young man that he was not hurt or offended. Then they suggested that I be called. The young man then called me.

This young man would have been doing exactly what the dominant culture has done — he would have been forcing people to do what they really didn't want to do. The gentleness of the Traditional Elders was a very good example.

I work together very closely with Traditional Elders. Every time we come together, we try to do things for the good of the community. We do things for the benefit of the people. We do things for the sake of God.

I think reconciliation may come to our communities if we respect each other and if we try to assist in understanding and not push our own way — a way which might not be comfortable. For some years there were many Pentecostal churches on the reserve. Now, there are only a few . . . and the Anglican church is growing stronger.

I worked at the Band Office for six years and now I work in vocational counselling. In my work, there is a stipulation that time may be taken for funerals and other services — so I am able to take time off — but still, my full-time work is not in the priesthood. This makes me sometimes feel that the people would be better served by a full-time priest.

I try to encourage all the people to assist with the church. I cannot drive people if they need to go to a hospital or to something in a city — but I know who may do those things. I try to draw on the strengths of the community and encourage people to help each other.

James Isbister
Sandy Lake/Ahtahkakoop Reserve,
Saskatchewan

Prayer for mediation
Creator God,
the leaders of the early Church were gentle,
not wishing to burden the people,
but leading them to Christ.

Give us understanding of your gracious love for all.
Let us be ever mindful of your intention for us,
that your way may be known upon all the earth.

May we enter your heavenly kingdom of light.

Prayer for all people
That we may be true to the word of God extending the
freedom and love of Christ to all, let us pray to the Lord.

SEVENTH SUNDAY OF EASTER

I will not leave you desolate, says the Lord; I will come to
you. *John 14.18*

Readings
Acts 16.16–34   *Psalm 97*
Revelation 22.12–14, 16–17, 20   John 16.20–26

In my grandmother's time, they always prayed to the Great
Spirit to look after them. I have sometimes wondered how
it was that they knew there was someone, some being,
looking after them. But they knew it.

I think sometimes of the Star, the Morningstar; how, in the
early days, they used to make the star quilt for the men,
and how they saw everything as sacred.

The quilt is patterned after the morning star. Just before
the first light of dawn there is a star in the east, just before
the colours of the new dawn begin to spread in the sky. It

is said that it is the brightest of all stars. This star most represents the Great Holy Spirit, shining through the darkness, greeting the first light.

My children now sometimes make the star quilts to sell. There are many who want to buy them. When they make them to sell, they make them of brightly coloured cotton broadcloth which they buy new in the store, not the scraps we used to use when we made them in the early days.

They are very beautiful — and even more beautiful when you think about their meaning. They have to be perfectly made so that all the pieces fit. Each piece must be perfectly cut, and all of them perfectly sewn together. And the whole pattern is like the light spreading in the early dawn, the colours of the dawn, with the star at the centre.

Many people like them. The people who admire and buy them, often ask, "What shall we do with such a beautiful quilt?" My children say, "Perhaps you could hang it on a wall — but whatever you do, you must use it to honour those you love."

Sometimes when I see the morning star and it seems to be so very bright, I don't feel surprised that the people saw this star as representing God. It is so bright just in the earliest hours of the day, just before the new day, and soft light begins to light the sky and touch the earth.

That is God. That is God being there for us. The Great Holy Spirit with us.

Jessie Saulteaux
Carry the Kettle,
Saskatchewan

Prayer for meditation

Creator,
we rejoice in your love.
You open prisons —
and guard the lives of the faithful.

You sent your angel to us
with the message that your Son, Jesus,
is the bright morning star.

You have loved us
before the foundation of the world.
May your love shine in us.

Prayer for all people

That understanding the love of Christ, we may be bearers
of his light and love in the world, let us pray to the Lord.

THE SEASON OF PENTECOST

Come, Holy Spirit, fill the hearts of your faithful; and kindle in us the fire of your love.

I remember my grandmother best with her arms upraised in prayer.

Once there was a storm coming — a great prairie storm. My grandmother went out to meet it. She stood before the storm with her arms held high and prayed to divide the storm.

I was a child then. It seemed to me as I watched, that it happened just this way — that the storm was divided by her prayer.

My mother had T.B. when I was young. She was expecting a baby again when I was twelve, and died of a heart attack. It was just too much for her; her heart gave out.

I remember although I was only twelve, on the evening she died, there was to be a pow-wow. When the people at the Y.M.C.A. hall learned of her death, they quit their pow-wow and most came to the house.

I saw them standing in a circle in starlight in front of the house, between twelve and two in the morning. They suddenly stopped talking — and it seemed as though the northern lights came closer and closer and reached down to where we were.

The beginning of the northern lights seemed to come right down and it was as though one could be carried on the light — and the men seemed to be following it south because they heard voices singing a pow-wow song.

I always remember that, how it happened that the northern lights came to our house that night.

My mother was forty-two when she died.

Jessie Saulteaux
Carry the Kettle,
Saskatchewan

PENTECOST

Come, Holy Spirit, fill the hearts of your faithful; and kindle in us the fire of your love.

Readings
Acts 1.1–21 or Genesis 11.1–9   Psalm 104.25–35
Romans 8.14–17 or Acts 2.1–21   John 14.8–17, 25–27

There is good and evil in every community. When I was a young child, I lost my mother. When my father remarried, my new mother had her own children. I was treated differently from her own.

When I was seventeen, I only wanted to be away. I believed that any place that I could go would be better than where I was. I found out that I was wrong. There is good and evil everywhere.

I felt that I was unlovable — unworthy of love. But, then I learned that I was loved by God — and I began to believe it.

My parents, like many other families, had moved into a community from settlements because of tuberculosis. There was much illness in the generation of my parents. When a family member was ill, the rest of the family moved to be close. And so everyone moved to a community.

My father had a job working for the Hudson's Bay. When I was a teenager, I worked for the Hudson's Bay as a clerk. Later, I trained as a technician and worked for many years for Bell Telephone. I flew so much that I had more hours on airplanes than anyone else in northern Quebec.

I had a good job and a high salary with lots of overtime. But our family was very concerned. There is much unhappiness among our people. My family and I prayed about what we could do to serve our people, to help them. After prayer, it was the decision of my whole family that I should become a priest.

I left my job and my community as well. I moved to Pang-nirtung to attend the Arthur Turner Training School to study to be a priest.

I'll never forget the day I was ordained priest. I was kneeling as hands were laid upon me. I felt the Holy Spirit come upon me — and I was completely changed. I will never be the same again. My whole family felt it as well. The power of God was so strong, we felt it so deeply in our hearts.

We have seven children. Two are our own — and five are adopted. My children are always bringing children home. Whey they know someone is being mistreated or abused, they bring them home. We try our best to care for them and to help them.

My wife and I both counsel people with problems — marital, spiritual, and physical problems. If a family is having a problem with alcohol or abuse, we try to see husband and wife and children — everybody together. If everyone is together, it is much easier to try to solve the problem. We get them to write down what they think is the problem. If it is written down, then we can communicate and share and try to solve the problems more easily.

Daniel Aupalu
Inukjuak, Ontario

Prayer for meditation
Lord of the oceans,
of all living things, great and small,
you touch the mountaintops,
you cause the earth to tremble,
your love surrounds all.

We are your children, your heirs,
co-heirs of your Kingdom with your Son, Jesus Christ.

131

May we be ever conscious of your Spirit of Truth
and share the peace which you have given
through the Holy Spirit, the advocate.

Prayer for all people
That all may be filled with the spirit of truth and know your
eternal kingdom, let us pray to the Lord.

TRINITY SUNDAY

Holy, holy, holy is the Lord of hosts; the whole earth is full
of his glory. *Isaiah 6.3*

Readings
Proverbs 8.22–31   *Psalm 8*
Romans 5.1–5   *John 16.12–15*

My grandfather is very wise. He's ninety-one years old —
and many come to him from quite far away.

There was a young boy named David, eight years old, who
came with his family looking for help with his cancer. He
was from a community very far north; he wasn't cured —
but he grew to love my grandfather.

As his cancer advanced, he was being treated in Montreal.
The doctors there told his family that there was no more
that they could do. When the boy understood that there
was no hope, he told his parents that he wished to be with
my grandfather. He told them that if he was with my
grandfather he would not be afraid of dying.

His parents used their last money to buy an air ticket to
visit my grandfather at our reserve. The family was not
wealthy. The father had quit his job with the band in order
to be with his child. They spent all their money coming to

our reserve — and they called my grandfather from the airport.

My grandfather called my mother. There was not enough room for the family with my grandfather and so we said of course they could stay with us.

We made a room for them, and made them welcome. They were a wonderful family. They had such love for their child — and they tried to do everything they could for him. They were so shy and humble — they didn't want to impose or put anybody out. They almost didn't want to eat so they wouldn't bother us.

The little boy didn't seem to talk very much but we didn't really know what was normal for him — so we didn't know how ill he really was. That night, he took a turn for the worse and we brought him and his family to the hospital. The nurses and doctors tried to make him comfortable. His mother and father stayed with him and we stayed with them also.

We got to know them so well; it seemed we had known them all our lives. We stayed with them at the hospital and when they came home from the hospital, my mother made them eat and tried to help them to talk.

The next night the parents were both so tired that the nurses said they should go back to our place and try to get some sleep. I drove them early the next morning. It was about a half hour to the hospital. Just after we left, a call came from the hospital that David had died.

We felt so badly that they hadn't been there with him when he died — after they had been so close to him and hadn't left him at all the whole time he'd been with us — but they seemed alright. In a way, they were comforting us. They had other young children — and they went ahead on the plane to be back with them. My mother and I and other members of my family helped in the preparations, made things nice and made things ready for his body to go back to his family.

It is strange how well we felt that we knew him. He was a beautiful little boy and it was such a difficult time for his family.

I am a child-care worker on my reserve. All this had happened over a weekend. I was so tired, and when I told the people at work what had happened over the weekend, they took up a collection for the family to help them with their expenses — and they told me to take some compassionate time off.

I was glad. I needed the time to grieve. When you are so close to people as they go through something like this, you feel such a loss yourself.

It was right, what we did, I am sure. I think God knows us well — and knows what we can take. My grandfather did what he could; we all did what we could to help them — and we will always feel close to their family.

Lana Grawbarger
Garden River, Ontario

Prayer for meditation
Creator God,
how majestic in all the earth is your name.
You have created all things,
the mountains, the fish of the seas, the birds of the air —
and in your wisdom we are created.

You shape us in your image.
We are complete in you.

Give us grace to answer the call of your voice.
May our hands be your hands on earth.
May we see the beauty of serving you in all ways.

Prayers for all people
That justified by faith, we may have peace with God
through our Lord Jesus Christ, let us pray to the Lord.

NINTH SUNDAY AFTER EPIPHANY
or between 29 May and 4 June

God so loved the world that he gave his only Son, that
whoever believes in him should not perish but have eternal
life. *John 3. 16*

Readings
1 Kings 8.22–23, 41–43   *Psalm 100*
Galatians 1.1–10   *Luke 7.1–10*

When I worked at an inner-city school for six years, it
started to bother me that with Native people, I could be
warm and friendly, but with white people, I backed away. I
was always afraid that they would say, "Get away from
me!"

I started a different job and I was still troubled by this
problem. I prayed about it. I remember putting on my
boots and praying, "God, you've always put me in jobs
where there's lots of problems, lots of alcoholism, people
hurting. God, you've got to help me — because I can't
comfort the white people. My love isn't strong enough. I
need your kind of love, the kind of love where I don't see
the difference between people."

Two weeks later, I went to some people's home. Something terrible had happened in their family. I cried with
them and comforted. They phoned me later, thanking me
for helping them.

I was telling this to the other staff people. When they

heard what had happened, they asked, "Is this a Native family?" I suddenly realized that I couldn't remember. I hadn't noticed whether they were Native or not. I said that I would find out and let them know.

I went to my office and sat there. I was numb. It just hit me what had happened. I couldn't remember if the people were black, white, or native. When I was in my office thinking about all these things by myself, it was as if I heard God saying, "I have answered your prayer." I said, "Oh! thank you God," and I started to cry. I was so moved! God answered my prayer — and I didn't even know it, didn't notice it was happening. I fell asleep in my chair and my phone rang beside me. I didn't hear it ringing. Finally, my husband came to my office door looking for me. He was worried because I always answered my phone. I was always home on time — and he wondered what had happened to me.

I learned two things from this. I learned that God answers prayer and I learned that it is important to be alone with God. We always have to take time no matter how busy we are to spend time alone with God.

Phyllis Keeper
Winnipeg, Manitoba/
Big Trout Lake, Ontario

Prayer for meditation
Creator, there is no God like you,
in heaven above or on earth below.

We worship you with gladness,
knowing that you made us and we are yours.

Your love endures forever,
your faithfulness extends to all.

Prayer for all people

That we may affirm the infinite varieties of ways that God calls men and women to be disciples, let us pray to the Lord.

SUNDAY BETWEEN 5 AND 11 JUNE

A great prophet has arisen among us! God has visited his people! *Luke 7.16*

Readings

1 Kings 17.17–24   Psalm 113
Galatians 1.11–24   Luke 7.11–17

In my community, I was always referred to as ''peeps.'' I was so small and so timid. I was shy and looked around corners, afraid to really join others, afraid to join a circle. I would stay back just a bit until I could feel comfortable. People would say, ''Oh, that's just like peeps!'' They would expect that of me.

I later joined the military. At first, I followed along with the crowd and I joined in the roughness and the drinking and the way we sometimes mistreated others in our uniforms — especially the women. I eventually became a Christian. I liked the military life — but I didn't like some parts of it and so I stopped doing the things I had been doing that sickened me after a while; so, I was sometimes persecuted by the others.

Eventually, though, they stopped deriding me. I was in parachuting and I did a very good job. I was respected for that. I did a lot of teaching and I am ashamed to say that sometimes it gave me pleasure when I would stand behind those husky young men in training and see them freeze.

137

Imagine that, I, a tiny man who had always been weak, would have to push them out of the plane — those husky men — to make them jump. Then, I would fail them when I got back to the ground.

I was married and after a few years I felt called to the priesthood. I think that I never did understand all of the things that happened. I ignored the call for as long as I could, but eventually I came to it.

It happened in this way. I was talking to Eddie, an Elder, and we were on our way to a pow wow. The grand entrance was just about to begin when I went up to him and said that I needed to talk to him.

''Come along,'' he said, and so I came with him. I was very moved when he told me to come along with him right then — he made the time for me. In my ministry now, when people ask for time, I often remember Eddie and how he spent that time with me.

We went off into the bush, and I told him how I had been struggling with this call to the ministry. He listened and then he drew on the ground a straight line. He pointed to one side of the line and then to the other. ''Two separate communities,'' he said, ''they have to find reconciliation, understanding.''

I looked and before my eyes he then drew a straight line connecting the two communities and I saw that what he had drawn was the shape of a cross.

''You have to find ways between those worlds,'' he said. ''Now, go back to the pow wow and enjoy yourself.''

That was how I finally felt affirmed in leaving the military and going back to school and taking theology to serve my people.

When I first went back to school at Emmanuel and St.

Chad after making my decision, I found that it was very hard. I came home from my first exam in English and found I had failed! I failed and wondered — why does God call me to do this?

Then my wife handed me a letter that someone had sent to me; it was a letter of encouragement and prayer. They didn't know that I had failed — but that letter came just at the right time. I decided then to go back. I took the course again. I passed it this time and went on to the other courses. I began in 1982 and graduated in 1988.

When I was ordained, I used the symbols of Native Tradition, and I was given a gift of a beadwork cross with a feather attached to it symbolizing the two ways coming together. On my ordination day, two little girls danced up the aisle with the elements held in their hands. It was very moving.

I work in urban Native ministry. I meet many people in the streets. I feel all of them have dignity, all of them have hope. I am always amazed how these people, who have so little, can offer so much hope to the rest of us.

Art Anderson
Regina/Kāneonuskatēw
(Gordon's Reserve),
Saskatchewan

Prayer for meditation
Creator,
from the rising of the sun to the setting,
we praise you.

Your hand is upon us.
You are our great prophet
who brings new life to us.

139

Lord, call us to new faith,
to new love, to new hope.

Prayer for all people

That the revelation of Christ may be proclaimed to all
people, let us pray to the Lord.

SUNDAY BETWEEN 12 AND 18 JUNE

In this is love, that God loved us and sent his Son to be
the expiation for our sins. *1 John 4.10*

Readings

1 Kings 19.1–8   Psalm 42
Galatians 2.15–21   Luke 7.36–8.3

I help at wakes and at graveside services; I help at baptisms. At church I help Sundays in pastoral prayer. Each
time I help in the church I am given added strength.

It is nice to know that people trust me — and people
depend on my prayer in hospitals, on reserves, and giving
communion.

It's a good life. Perhaps people say I'm not playing a good
role but I know the King knows my heart — and God will
forgive me if I'm doing wrong. I serve God in my own
Anishinabe way doing what I think I should be doing.

I thank God for the strength I've been given when I ask for
rest in the night. If I didn't do that — I don't know where
I'd be.

You don't need to pray out loud — but kneel to pray. There
are no secrets where God is. Just say a prayer — because
God is only a breath away and He won't let you down.

In life, we never know whether we are going to make it through the day, but we live in hope that when the time comes we will hear Him, and He will say "Your work's done — come home and rest now."

I don't think He'll talk to me in a language I don't understand, because he gave us each a language — and I'm proud to use mine.
I'll still be able to maintain my Ojibwa language.

Gladys Taylor
Curve Lake, Ontario

Prayer for meditation
As a deer longs for flowing streams,
   so my soul longs for you, O God.
Psalm 42.1

Creator,
your Son in his life on earth
reached out to all —
to a woman in tears at his feet.

We long to know your love.
May we understand and receive your boundless love,
serving each other gladly,
with graciousness and care.

Prayer for all people
That we may understand Christ lives in us and we are accepted and justified in every culture through faith in Christ, let us pray to the Lord.

NATIVE DAY OF PRAYER — *June 21*

June 21, the summer solstice and day of longest light, is recognized as a Native Day of Prayer. There are many

141

prayer vigils and fasts during that time. The following is an overview of Christian and Native traditions. Readers may find this overview by Traditional leader William Dumas to be useful for reflection, teaching, or for personal preparation for the Day of Prayer.

All religions have two things in common: theology and ritual. Theology is what we believe. It describes the laws that form our religious beliefs. Ritual is something done within the Church or Tradition. It is a ceremony.

In the Christian religion, the word we use to describe God is Jesus Christ. In Native Tradition, the word we use is *Kise Manitou* meaning Great Spirit. Our people have always known that there is a God, a head figure.

The Cross is a symbol representing the death of Christ, and by that we are saved from eternal damnation. The Sacred Pipe, the Peace Pipe, has the same symbolism in Traditional ways.

Christians pray through the Cross. Native Traditional people pray through the Sacred Pipe. The Pipe is the medium between you and the Creator. After the Pipe is passed, unity comes and people can talk.

The Church, especially the Catholic church, has its saints and angels. There are patron saints, guardian saints, who speak on one's behalf to God. In Native Tradition, PAWAKAN are spirits, relatives, who come to us in dreams; sometimes, we can see that spirit.

In the Church, we have confessionals, times when we are purified, cleansed of sin, forgiven. In Native Tradition, we go for this cleansing to the sweat lodge. The sweat lodge is in the Earth, our mother. It is in the shape of a pregnant woman and when you go into the sweat lodge, it is like going back into the womb in your mind. You ask for the

Creator's forgiveness — and you leave all the bad things inside the sweat lodge. When you leave the sweat lodge through the small opening, you are like a small child, reborn, cleaned, and healed.

In the Christian Church, incense is used and smudged. It is sweet smelling and clears the air so that prayers may be sent in a clear path. Sweetgrass is used in Traditional ways. When smudging is done at ceremonies or alone at home, it clears the air of the negative energy around us. Then, the door to your mind and heart is opened and you can talk to your Creator. (Sweetgrass is new in some communities where it doesn't grow.)

If one studies Native spirituality and Christian, one will find a lot of similarities. Don't get confused with stories of Weesakajak. This is a different category of story. This is a legend.

It takes a lot of work to study Native Traditional ways. There are some who would like to become ''instant medicine men.'' They think they have learned something — and they see themselves as medicine men — but they often end up being lost. Don't try to become instant medicine men and women. It takes years of training with the Elders to learn these things. It takes time, study — and understanding of truth. I pray in sweat lodges. I am a Pipe carrier. These are things one has to earn.

If, after time and study, one is able to put together the importance of love, respect, faith, and peace with humility, one will find all those ingredients in Native Spiritual Traditions. They are all there.

William Dumas
South Indian Lake/
Thompson, Manitoba

143

SUNDAY BETWEEN 19 AND 25 JUNE

My sheep hear my voice, says the Lord; I know them and they follow me. *John 10.27*

Readings
1 Kings 19.9–14 *Psalm 43*
Galatians 3.23–29 *Luke 9.18–24*

I was very loved by my parents. In the Inuit culture a girl is often married young. If a child is born soon, the family of the wife will take that child. My older brother was cared for by my grandparents. After that a child was born who didn't live. I was the third child and when I was born, my mother was a little older and looking forward to my birth.

There was a great tragedy in the family of my father. He had a wife and five children who died together in an epidemic. After this, my father married my mother.

Marriage in our culture is often misunderstood. For example, we have had a custom of arranged marriages. Outsiders have not understood that this was necessary for survival. A woman had to have a good hunter for a husband. If a man was not a good hunter, his family might starve. A man had to have a woman who would work hard to care for the family. It would appear to outsiders to be a very bad thing, a couple forced to marry against their own wishes.

Survival of the culture demanded that the family unit be strong. Parents did their best to find good partners for their children. Times have changed very much. Parents no longer can tell their children what they should do and whom they should marry.

Children want to make up their own minds and make their own decisions. And so they do. But, when the young couple have problems, their parents are bewildered and do not know how to help them learn to get along and love each other. It is a problem.

In one generation people have moved from the land to settlements. When they give up the old way of life on the land, they give up more than they thin'...
world, our language is filled w'...
should not be lost and in m...
been lost. People don't reali...
guage is lost because it is a... ...u relationship to
the land.

It is very important to keep this in mind; there are many problems when we think we must give up language which describes the land and the place we live. Language describes relationships with animals and the hunting life. All this goes together with the way of life. It is very hard to translate some things. There are no English words for some of the things which we would wish to describe. This is because with another language, the way of life is different and does not depend on the closeness to the land and the understanding of the land in order to survive as it does in our culture.

We must find ways in our faith to help our people adjust to the changes without losing identity. If I did not have Christ, I don't know what I would do. Christ is the rock I depend upon.

Andrew Atagotaluk
Pond Inlet,
Northwest Territories

Prayer for meditation
O Lord,
like the mighty prophets of old —
may we listen to your voice
— a voice coming in silence
after the mighty wind and the great earthquake
and the fire.

Your voice comes in the stillness of our hearts,
bringing light and truth,
leading us to your dwelling place. .

Like Peter, may we look up
and see "The Christ of God."

Through the love of your Son Christ,
may we experience true freedom in your love,
trusting in you always.

Prayer for all people
That we may all see ourselves as children of God through
faith, understanding that the Spirit of his Son is in our
hearts, let us pray to the Lord.

SUNDAY BETWEEN 26 JUNE AND 2 JULY

Speak Lord, for your servant is listening: you have the
words of eternal life. *See 1 Samuel 3.9; John 6.68*

Readings
1 Kings 19.15–21   Psalm 44.1–8
Galatians 5.1, 13–25   Luke 9.51–62

Today, wherever you go, wherever you turn around, there
are people drinking.

I didn't know what to do when it first started to happen to
my husband. I talked to the minister and to the farm
instructor, too. They didn't seem to have any help. The
minister said I might go to the owner of the hotel and tell
him about it — and he would put a person on the black
list. I would have to have a good reason to do this.

I don't know what he meant by this. Did it mean if a man

is neglecting his family or beating his wife or family? There were many who did beat their wives when liquor was open to Indians. I was not beaten. Around the time that I would be putting children to bed there would be visitors. There was one room in the house and on one side of the room were the visitors; on the other side of the room I was reading Bible stories and Sunday School papers to the children as I was putting them to bed.

But, he didn't go for liquor until he had what we needed for groceries. The children always had food. The liquor — he would get it from white friends who would come with favours.

It is strange how a man, when drinking, will sometimes laugh and cry — and pray. He was a hard worker and a good gardener. At that time groceries were cheap and he was generous with his garden and with his working for others. He won many prizes for gardening. He often gave money — but it was hard to talk to him. It was always hard to talk to him about many things — especially about alcohol — what it was doing to his mind and to his body.

On his side, there was no one to say the kinds of things that my grandmother taught us although there were some good things he was taught. I remember his father holding our oldest daughter when she was only three and saying, "This is a precious child of God in your home, and you must look after her. When you have a child like this, be good to her and don't treat her rough because she is sacred. She must learn how to look after her own life."

This which his father taught is the same he now teaches with his own grandchildren.

Every now and then I remember him giving that advice to his own boys. He also told them, "It's hard to go through life. You're going to meet bad times, bad friends. Don't fight or hold a grudge. When that happens, if someone should hit on one side of the face, show them the other side of your face. Don't fight.'' He also says to always remember they have a home.

Jessie Saulteaux
Carry the Kettle,
Saskatchewan

Prayer for meditation
Creator God,
we have heard what our ancestors told us,
the light of your countenance was upon them.

We trust in you.
Grant us grace, and when we meet discouragement
may we know your love surrounding and upholding us.

As we build a new future,
may we look to the light of your love
to guide us ever on the way.

Prayer for all people
That we may live by the Spirit, and led by the Spirit not submit to the yoke of slavery, but inherit the Kingdom of God, let us pray to the Lord.

SUNDAY BETWEEN 3 AND 9 JULY

Let the peace of Christ rule in your hearts; let the word of Christ dwell in you richly. *Colossians 3.15, 16*

Readings
1 Kings 21.1–3, 17–21   *Psalm 5.1–8*
Galatians 6.7–18   *Luke 10.1–12, 17–20*

I took chaplaincy training for eighteen months.

When I went home for the funeral of my brother, I was tired and discouraged. I didn't realize how tired I was, but I sat there with people around me. People talked to me — and I think I understood and answered — but I really wasn't listening. I was just fed up. Everywhere I looked, there were people drunk — my people drunk! I didn't want to see them anymore, always drinking and hurting each other.

I have always served people. They always seemed to come to me for help. They came to me at Christmas, they came to me at Easter. They always came to me. My house was always big enough. I was always doing something for people — and people didn't even ask me if I wanted a cup of tea.

My brother had drowned and I didn't even want to go and see his body. I was sitting in my sister-in-law's house. My mother had adopted a boy who was much younger than the rest of us. Many of us were staying in this brother's home. They had a young son about three years old.

It was winter and the little boy was struggling to get on his snowsuit. Different people wanted to help him, but his mother said, "No, let him do it himself. He likes to do it himself — and he will be happy when he does it himself." He struggled and struggled and then finally he got it on! He was all dressed up, ready to go outside. He was going to go sledding.

It was taking quite a long time for the rest of us to get ready for prayers. The little boy pulled on his mother's skirt and asked, "Prayer? We say prayer?" When he said that, the feelings I had as a little girl came back.

Suddenly I thought, "This is how I grew up! From the time we were little, this is how we lived. We didn't go anywhere, we didn't do anything — even go outside without saying our prayers first.'' I looked at that little boy and I saw how beautiful he was. God opened my eyes and I saw how beautiful that way of life was. I remembered the good things — and I saw how beautiful my own people were.

The funeral was a beautiful funeral and we had to walk a long way through the bushes to and from the church. We walked and walked and as we walked different people joined us and everyone was singing hymns.

This is something I needed to have happen to me. I had grown away from my people as they lived on my reserve. For years I had worked with the people of the north end of Winnipeg and the core area of Winnipeg. In my work and in chaplaincy training, I worked with people who had problems of poverty, alcoholism, and family breakdown. I was beginning to think of my people as people who always needed things.

I suddenly saw how beautiful the people were. I could see the beauty of my people in a new way. Then I noticed that they were saying, ''Phyllis, come for tea, Phyllis, drop by and visit.'' It was as though I was hearing them say this for the first time, too.

God filled me up. I saw my people in a different way. I appreciated the things that are good in the Indian way of life. This has stayed with me in my ministry. I still enjoy and see people in this way now.

Phyllis Keeper
Winnipeg, Manitoba/
Big Trout Lake, Ontario

Prayer for meditation
Creator,
you have set your glory above the heavens,
out of the mouths of children you teach us.

You have created everything —
birds of the air, the fish of the lakes and streams and seas.
Your name is wonderful.

Give us grace to see anew the wonders of your creation.
May we be refreshed in our hearts
and renewed in our souls.

Prayer for all people
That we may not grow weary in doing good, but grow in
the grace of Christ, let us pray to the Lord.

SUNDAY BETWEEN 10 AND 16 JULY

The words you have spoken are spirit and life, O Lord; you
have the words of eternal life. *See John 6.63, 83*

Readings
2 Kings 2.1, 6–14   *Psalm 139.1–11*
Colossians 1.1–14   *Luke 10.25–37*

Our task is proclaiming and preaching and helping others to
be servants of God. The Church has to be a servant
Church. We are called to give up our lives in the service of
others. In Matthew 20.20, the mother of two of the disciples, the sons of Zebedee, asked if her children could have
a special place in heaven. There are no special seats in
heaven. All our ministries are valid.

What is ministry? There are many ministries for us. Wherever we are is our ministry. Christ made it clear that one is
not to lord it over others — but to serve. Love the Lord
your God — and your neighbour as yourself.

Who is my neighbour? Christ was very clear on who one's
neighbour is as well. Ministry is service: the sad thing is

that clergy and people believe that ministry is for the clergy.

Every person in the Church is a minister. I remember a man who was working as a fork-lift operator in a factory. When he went to work, many were rough and took the Lord's name in vain. When the man heard this, he began to pray for them. After awhile, others noticed his example — and the whole workplace was changed because of his example. He was a minister where he was. We should all remember that in the work that we do God calls us to be servants.

In a service once, I asked people to place on the altar the symbol of their ministries. I recall the symbols of three women: the first was a copy of *The Sacrifice*, brought to the altar by an English teacher, a profound story which symbolized what she does in her daily teaching. The second was a hand-made porcupine quill basket. This woman had crafted beautiful baskets and this was her offering of herself to God. The third woman placed on the altar her car keys. At that time in her life, she was spending a goodly amount of time driving her children to the many activities in their lives — and so her time in driving was her offering to God, her ministry of nurture.

As leaders, we must ask the question: How can we help the people of God to see their daily work as ministry?

Walter Jones
Winnipeg, Manitoba

Prayer for meditation
Creator God,
you are around us, you are within us.
Wherever we are, you are with us.

If we rise on the wings of morning to farthest lakes and seas,
your hand leads us and holds us.

May we reach out to all around us,
growing strong, patiently working, giving thanks
for the Kingdom of your beloved Son, Jesus Christ our
Lord.

Prayer for all people
That we may be filled with the knowledge of God's will in
all spiritual wisdom and understanding, leading lives dedicated to the Lord, let us pray to the Lord.

SUNDAY BETWEEN 17 AND 23 JULY

Blessed are they who hold the word fast in an honest and
good heart, and bring forth fruit with patience.
See Luke 8.15

Readings
2 Kings 4.8–17   Psalm 139.12–17
Colossians 1.21–29   Luke 10.38–42

I am grateful to be part of this gathering. The women
helpers — who are they? The Church is in each settlement
and we, the women, are the helpers.

We have been given power by Jesus Christ — not only for
serving things — but for worshipping together. We also
have Bible studies to learn more about God's words.

Some of our older women who have been good and faithful helpers of the A.E. have passed away. It is our understanding as women that we should teach in our own
communities and help if someone is in need.

We try hard to explain that we as Anglicans try to work
together. We try to work hard. The Church should try to
work hard and be able to serve all people no matter who

they are. If this could be done, it would be great because we all have to work together in the same way.

Our responsibility is great but it is important for us to know that we are supported by the whole community. The annual report of each community is important to me. Prayer support is important to all of us. All A.E.s want to have a closer relationship with vestries and support each other more. We need to keep communication between different A.E. groups as well.

I have also a concern that people in the communities may want to provide help — but it is too much for us as members to respond to all needs. At times, we are abused as members. We must use the resources of the A.E. in a right way. We have a concern with the cleaning of houses. We organize and help those who do not have anyone to help them. It looks now as though the A.E. may be used for almost anything. Our work of the A.E. is being taken advantage of.

Therefore I want to ask you to do all you can to help us so that we may do as Paul in Romans 16 suggested: "Phoebe our sister . . . also helps many." We wish to be a help — but we wish not to be abused and asked to do so much that we cannot care for our own families.

Meeka Arnakak*
Pangnirtung, Northwest Territories

Prayer for meditation
Creator,
the darkness is not dark to you —
the night is as bright as the day.

You formed us and know us well.

We are tired, Lord.
The needs are great, the workers few.

Grant us peace, Lord,
and stillness of heart in our service to you.

May we rest at your feet for awhile.

Prayer for all people
That reconciled in the body of Christ, holy and blameless,
we may live in all wisdom, let us pray to the Lord.

SUNDAY BETWEEN 24 AND 30 JULY

When we cry, "Abba, Father!" it is the Spirit of God bearing witness with our spirit that we are the children of God.
Romans 8.15,16

Readings
2 Kings 5.1–15ab ("'. . . in Israel")   Psalm 21.1–7
Colossians 2.6–15   Luke 11.1–13

---

* Meeka Arnakak is President of the Eastern Region for Agnait Ikayuktiu-
katauyun (referred to as A.E. and translated as women who work
together). This is the Inuktitut version of the Anglican Church Women.
The above is a response in part to concerns expressed from branches of
A.E. at Synod of the Arctic in 1990. John R. Sperry, retired bishop of
the Arctic, outlines that "the references to 'abuse' and 'being taken
advantage of' has to do with communities thinking that any dirty job is
better left to a women's organization or, individuals trying to get finances
from A.E. accounts." Ms. Arnakak provided an insight into the pressures
women in communities across the Arctic are facing. Survival of the Inuit
culture in a harsh environment required unusual strength of the family
unit. Rapid social change in the North has resulted in high incidence of
family breakdown and substance abuse. Leaders in communities, many
of them women, struggle with trying to provide care to many. In
response to the report by Ms. Arnakak, Bishop Sperry affirmed the
importance of the work of the women in the diocese — and the need to
support their work.

When my grandmother died, I couldn't be home. I always remember how I wanted to be home, how I longed to be home at that time.

At the time of the opening of the training centre for Native theological students, I was standing at the ceremony, and it seemed to me that I saw a clear light around the people in the ceremony. I was expecting that they might ask me to speak — but they didn't. And then later on I saw many little lights — and I think that those lights are like many little stars and those lights are the lights of our young people as they begin to take training and become leaders in our communities.

At the time of the ceremony, I didn't say anything, but I hoped that over time, we would find that we were doing the right thing, by finding ways to bring leadership training to our own people. A few times, it just about seemed to fall apart. A few times, it seemed that people were saying we shouldn't be trying to do this on our own, we shouldn't be trying to do our own training.

We have to be guided by someone, by somebody. So, with the help of our ministers, we have come this far — and we are going into a brighter future. All those little stars are going to get bigger, they are going to shine brighter. There are going to be more and more leaders.

God is always there to know what we are doing. I remember the first pictures I saw in Sunday School. There was a picture of Christ with all the little children. Then there was another with him again, being a shepherd. Those pictures were important although we didn't speak English. By looking at those pictures, we knew what they meant. After going to school, I knew the words to the pictures. But the pictures alone were enough to understand.

Dr. Jessie Saulteaux
Carry the Kettle, Saskatchewan

Prayer for meditation
Creator,
We rejoice in your strength,
you bestow blessings upon us,
making us glad in your presence.

We come to you with our need,
knowing you will answer.
We try again and again to follow your word,
knowing our desire will be honoured.

Grant that guided by your love
we may believe in ourselves, holding ever before us,
the picture of you, our great Shepherd
going before us, leading us into a brighter future.

Prayer for all people
That we may continue rooted in Christ, abounding in
thanksgiving, let us pray to the Lord.

SUNDAY BETWEEN 31 JULY AND 6 AUGUST

Blessed are the poor in spirit, for theirs is the kingdom of
heaven. *Matthew 5.3*

Readings
2 Kings 13.14–20a   *Psalm 28*
Colossians 3.1–11   *Luke 12.13–21*

A vision is a way the spirit comes into our lives from time
to time to give us direction.

I was once involved in a project to evaluate graduates of a
program which attempted to reintegrate youth, who had
been incarcerated, back into the community. Together with
other members of the project, I was travelling through

rolling hills north of Toronto to a retreat centre. We had talked quite a bit of the time. Then, we had a long spell when we were quiet. There was a full moon and you could see everything outside clearly. I was sitting in the back seat, looking back to where we had come from. I had an incredibly strong feeling that I had been this way before — and that I would soon be living in the area. It was a very peaceful feeling, a settling feeling.

About three months later, I applied for a position as minister in the small community of Tottenham. It was only after I was settled there for three months that I remembered the vision I'd had on that fall night which told me I would be coming to live in the area.

This is an example of how vision is a common everyday experience — if we are open to acknowledging the presence of the spirit in that way.

The vision quest that we talk about in Native Traditional ways can come at a specific period in a young person's life — and is part of a process of coming into adulthood and discovering what the spirit has for you to do in this life. There is a time when you go into the wilderness or apart from the community so you can be alone with yourself — without all the distractions that come with community life.

The vision experience is something that continues to happen throughout one's life, and can occur either in the community or by purposefully setting aside time to go off from the community.

From all my study of the Old and New Testaments, and what I have gleaned from the Traditional community, there doesn't seem a great difference in the questing. The questing is trying to find out what God is saying to us in the midst of our time.

The other part of vision which is equally important as

having the vision is *testing the vision*. The Old and New Testament teach that all visions have to be tested with reality. So, we bring our vision back and live out our vision. If our vision is true, it will be seen as a gift brought to the whole community. If our vision is false, then it will bear no fruit at all. That is one of the things that one has to be aware of in understanding visioning.

The biblical teaching is: by their works, you shall know them.

Alf Dumont
Winnipeg, Manitoba/
Shawanaga, Ontario

Prayer for meditation
Creator,
we lift ourselves to your holy sanctuary;
you are our strength, our shepherd who carries us forever.

When we are caught up with earthly matters,
grant us places of stillness and silence.

May we hear your call.

Prayer for all people
That we may set our minds on things of Christ, let us pray to the Lord.

SUNDAY BETWEEN 7 AND 13 AUGUST

Watch and be ready, for you do not know on what day your Lord is coming. *Matthew 24.42, 44*

Readings
Jeremiah 18.1–11   *Psalm 14*
Hebrews 11.1–3, 8–19   *Luke 12.32–40*

I never take the time to think about myself — I'm always too busy looking after others. I don't take the time to consider myself because of my busyness. I keep on doing the things I do and don't take the time for myself. Since my ordination in 1986, I can relate to what Psalm 139 is saying: *Lord, you examine me, you know me.*

I haven't been a good steward to my family. In my full-time job, I have to share with my people. I share the money, and what little is left goes to my family. I expect them to see what I do — and respect and understand this. I expect this especially of my wife, the one I'm closest to.

What the psalmist says in Psalm 139 has touched the inner part of my person. I have to somehow match what is on the inside and what is on the outside. I understand from what the psalmist says that one has to take the opportunity to heal all things — not just heal the whole body of Christ, but heal ourselves as well.

A lot of times, we forget that we also need time, and don't take the time for ourselves and family. Whatever is left over is for ourselves and our family. That's what I do.

It is difficult to really know that God is there for us every day of our lives. I thought that when we have a commitment, we have to give totally — but I have had a problem. I give of myself too much. I see instead that when we are committed, we must also look after ourselves.
Where this understanding now is, there was a blank before. As I talk and consider this passage, it gives me what I need to work on and that is myself — especially now. On my reserve, I am dealing with abuse of all kinds. As it begins to be talked about, it starts a chain reaction. A person who was ''born again'' was molesting his daughters. Another neighbour — I didn't know the things that were happening in his home. All the other things around

us, that we didn't know were happening, are suddenly being opened up.

I always did everything by myself — but now, I know I must be first in the recuperation process. It can be a very important and healing process to think of oneself and to think of one's family. I am working with vestry and they're saying very clearly — "Think of yourself." It's hard to do this being Native because the Elders say "You don't think of yourself."

In sharing these thoughts, I understand that this is where we get the power and the strength to continue. I can relate to most of the things the psalmist was saying in Psalm 139. I understand I have to be complete in myself first before I can really be effective.

We are all equal and each of us has something to share. In ourselves, we don't have the power, but with the prayer and faith of others, we have the power to carry on and to continue to learn and to grow.

James Isbister
Sandy Lake/Ahtahkakoop Reserve, Saskatchewan

Prayer for mediation
Creator,
on every side there are problems, demands.
We are torn by the need.

Quiet our hearts,
teach us your ways
that we may find peace in you.

Lord, may we examine ourselves,
care for our homes and families,
allow ourselves to be ministered to,
that we, our families, and our communities
may be brought to fuller life in you.

Prayer for all people

That by faith we may understand our hope and inheritance to be founded upon the word of God and that that word calls us to care for ourselves, let us pray to the Lord.

SUNDAY BETWEEN 14 AND 20 AUGUST

My sheep hear my voice, says the Lord; I know them and they follow me. *John 10.27*

Readings

Jeremiah 20.7–13   Psalm 10.12–19
Hebrews 12.1–2, 12–17   Luke 12.49–56

Not long ago, there was a rebirth of Native Spiritual Traditions. There are a lot of prophesies that talk about how the Indian will come alive again. Black Elk saw his people crying and he said it will take five generations before the Indian people will start living again: we are the fifth generation.

There are many good things happening. It is our duty to help make these things happen. To do this, keep listening to the light inside your head. That light is called knowledge. Knowledge will drive away fear.

There is a teaching called The Peace Tree in Mohawk tradition. In the west it is called the medicine wheel.

When you look at a tree, one of the things you notice is that for every year of growth there is a ring, a circle. Eventually it becomes big and strong. Knowledge becomes a part of each of us and as we grow stronger, it gets bigger. Everything around becomes a part of us and becomes bigger.

In the beginning, you start from the east where the sun comes up. You have to know that in a holistic way of living, all learning begins in the east. Each direction represents a part of how we become persons. The north represents how we think, the east represents our physical persons, the south is our emotional being — feelings and emotions — and the west represents our soul, what we cannot see, but everyone has.

The physical is part of the emotional is part of the spiritual is part of the mental. Everything works together and we have to find a balance. When one of these suffers, everything suffers.

When I was a boy, through learning, I understood that this whole thing becomes a part of one's psyche. It's quite an awesome thing. If you understand how you are made, then that knowledge becomes your protection.

Sometimes there is social pressure in communities, and people can be destroyed by that. When I was little, there was someone who had a problem. In the community, they said, "Look, someone has done something wrong and is being punished" — and there was fear that maybe this was something evil, that someone had done some bad medicine.

I went to the nurse — and I asked, "What happened? Is this bad medicine?" "No," she said, "that person has had a stroke." Then she explained how the blood goes to a certain part of the head and causes damage and it is hard for the person to talk. I understood it then. I was no longer afraid. Knowledge is important. Keep on learning, keep on studying.

Don't be afraid to ask questions.

William Dumas
Thompson/South Indian Lake
Manitoba

163

Prayer for meditation

Rise up, O Lord; O God, lift up your hand;
> do not forget the oppressed.

>> *Psalm 10*

O Lord, everywhere there is violence and destruction.
But, you test the righteous,
you see the heart and mind.

May we have the courage to look at ourselves,
to try new understandings, new ways,
to pursue peace and holiness.

Prayer for all people

That we may run with perseverance the race set before us,
looking to Jesus, the perfecter of our faith, let us pray to
the Lord.

SUNDAY BETWEEN 21 AND 27 AUGUST

I am the way, the truth and the life, says the Lord; no one
comes to the Father but by me. *John 14.6*

Readings

Jeremiah 28.1–9   *Psalm 84*
Hebrews 12.18–29   *Luke 13.22–30*

The Church is not just a group of people, but a group of
people who are working for God. The Bible speaks of the
Christian as the salt of the earth. Salt is used in two ways:
it is used to keep things from spoiling, and it is used to
give taste. Just as the salt makes food taste good, we are

to be a help wherever we can; and just as salt stops food from spoiling, we are to bring peace on earth.

Johnston Garrioch
Cross Lake, Manitoba

It is important to remember that the apology was acknowledged, but not accepted. We would appreciate the Church putting action to their words just as we as Native people must put action to ours.

Here are the issues that we in the Council of Healing are talking about; we must walk hand in hand to start understanding each other and how we can work together to bring about change.

We advocate the right to be distinct people with different cultures and spiritual beliefs. We wish to become self-determining people. We must ask ourselves the question: what are the specific issues we can start working on ourselves?

We must restore pride and human dignity. We want to be equal. We must resist any laws, practices, and policies to assimilate Native people. We must start publicizing Native concerns.

We must continue supporting our Native brothers and sisters through providing resource material, developing videos, and having more dialogue within the churches.

We need to start with our own churches, to tell our own struggles and stories, so we bring understanding of Native issues. There is a lot of sympathy for Native issues — but we need to harness that and educate people to know how to assist.

There is a need for development of pamphlets, books, and resources.

165

As individuals coming from where we come, a lot of us face different problems in our communities.

We must start in our own backyards to heal ourselves.

Samuel Bull
Goodfish Lake, Alberta

Prayer for meditation
How lovely is your dwelling place,
    O Lord of hosts!
Psalm 84

Creator,
the sparrows find a home,
the swallows find a nest.

We look for the prophet of peace,
we look for honesty and integrity.

May we take responsibility in our lives,
living with discipline, meaning, hope, and commitment.

You are our sun and our shield.

Prayer for all people
That we may know our faith to rest truly in Jesus, whose Kingdom cannot be shaken, and who is the mediator of the New Covenant.

SUNDAY BETWEEN 28 AUGUST AND 3 SEPTEMBER

Take my yoke upon you, and learn from me; for I am gentle and lowly in heart. *Matthew 11.29*

Readings
Ezekiel 18.1–9, 25–29   Psalm 15
Hebrews 13.1–8   Luke 14.1, 7–14

When missionaries came to my community, my parents decided to become Anglican. I grew up in the Anglican church. In those days, the only education we could get was through the Anglican church. St. Peter's was the church we went to. When I was ten, my parents decided to send my brother and me away to school. This was a wrenching decision and it was made because my parents felt that the day school we attended was not up to par with other schools in B.C.

I wasn't taken away, as many were, to go to residential school. It was the choice of my parents. My father was a hereditary chief and he was involved in the issue of land claims. He felt that the only way our people could get justice from the white people was if we learned their system. This was why my brother and I were sent to residential school. At the school, where we were, we were treated with kindness. It was a United Church school and they taught me many things. I learned their ways. When it was time to go to high school, I returned to my community.

I wasn't active in the Church in my late teens. Like many other teens, I drew away from it. All this time my parents were very faithful members. I married out of my culture, and it wasn't until I began to have children that I understood how much I had had in the Anglican church — and I wanted this for my children as well. My husband was raised in the United church and he was supportive of what I did. I gave him a choice to take the children to the United church, but he said, "No — your church is very important to you and you should take them to the Anglican church."

I have been active at the parish level and held every office in the A.C.W. on the parish level. When the children grew up I became active on the diocesan level. I am now vice-president of the diocesan A.C.W. Over the years I've missed very few of the annual meetings of the A.C.W.

When the children grew up, I wanted to do something different from what I had been doing. I was well supported by my husband, and I didn't need to work, but I wanted to do something for myself. At this time our Tribal Council was looking for researchers to assist them in their negotiations for land rights.

In the job, age was no obstacle — and the ability to speak the language was necessary. I felt, at first, reluctant. Then I felt very strongly, as I have felt many times in my life, that this was a job God wished me to have.

I worked for four years as a researcher and during that time it was my job to speak to Elders and to tape their stories, translate them, and then place them on computer. A very exciting part of the job for me was that I found that what the Elders said, I already knew. I must have been listening more than I thought when I was a child — but somehow I had to hear someone else say it before I knew it was right.

Another very important thing was learning how the Native Traditional beliefs and the teachings of the Church went together. Traditional knowledge and what we heard in church seemed to blend so very well — and this surprised me. Since then I've read so many books on anthropology and there are many more to read. I learned that we as Native people are very important. I believe we are very important in the Church as well. These things seem to go together, my work as a researcher and my work in the Church.

Around this time I began to be more involved in the Anglican church at the diocesan level. I heard my bishop once and he was saying, ''Quit fooling around with your faith and prove you mean what you're saying.'' I took that as a challenge. I stopped refusing requests to be involved at the diocesan level. I often had refused because I felt that others would be more capable than I would be.

I've been to Provincial Synod. I served on the national level on the Women's Unit. I enjoy serving on the Women's Unit. I get to know many women and often younger women. I have also gone to the Council of the North conference in Vancouver with my bishop and that was an opportunity of a lifetime, an exciting time to meet many people and learn how northern dioceses function. That is also how I came to be involved on the Native Convocation task force.

On a personal note, I have raised nine children. I now have twenty-two grandchildren and every one of them is precious to me. And I want to say that this is where my hope is. One of the things that we believe where I come from is that when we come to the end of our time on earth — we leave a bit of our energy here. I hope that when I leave, I will leave with my grandchildren a little bit of what's good in my life — and the Church has been very important to the way I look at things and the way I respond to people. My great hope for the future lies in my grandchildren. I hope that I will have passed on my respect for all of God's creation of life, including one's own life and the responsibility that goes with the respect.

Vi Smith
Hazelton/
Gitanmaax, B.C.

Prayer for meditation
Creator,
all our lives are yours.

We are responsible for our own life.
Your pleasure is that we live in righteousness.

We give thanks for opportunities
to grow in understanding and offer our gifts
to your service.

May we speak the truth in love from our hearts,
learning and growing together as your community.

Prayer for all people
That with the Lord as our helper, we may grow in mutual
love, sharing, and hospitality, let us pray to the Lord.

SUNDAY BETWEEN 4 AND 10 SEPTEMBER

Let your countenance shine upon your servant and teach
me your statutes. *Psalm 119.135*

Readings
Ezekiel 33.1–11   *Psalm 94.12–22*
Philemon 1.20   *Luke 14.25–33*

I am in a Native congregation. When I am at church, I am
always doing this and doing that. I am always busy.

As part of my training for ordination, I spent six months in
another parish. There, the people weren't Native. I joined
them for Bible study.

On one night we were meeting and the church was cold.
One of the people said, "Oh, the church is too cold, let's
go over to my house."

So we went over to her house. When it was time for tea, I
jumped up to help. "Relax, Phyllis," she said, "sit down
and relax." She brought me a cup of tea and it was like

receiving Holy Communion. I wanted to cry so much. I didn't get up, I didn't help wash up. I just sat there — and for me, that cup was really shining.

I thought to myself, "What did they put in that tea? Some kind of drug?" I realized that I have to accept things from other people.

I look for God's presence in every experience. I am told that when I prepare sermons, I shouldn't rely on my own experience — but when you look for God's presence, you find that God is always there. You never run out of experiences. He's right there, shining his light.

Phyllis Keeper
Winnipeg, Manitoba/
Big Trout Lake, Ontario

Prayer for meditation
Creator,
your steadfast love upholds us.
When our cares are many,
your consolation cheers our souls.

May we be willing to receive,
to accept the gracious offerings of others.
May we see your presence everywhere.

Prayer for all people
That we may accept each other as true brothers and sisters, giving and receiving freely, let us pray to the Lord.

SUNDAY BETWEEN 11 AND 17 SEPTEMBER

There is joy before the angels of God over one sinner who repents. *Luke 15.10*

Readings

Hosea 4.1–3; 5.15–6.6   *Psalm 77.11–20*
1 Timothy 1.12–17   *Luke 15.1–10*

My grandmother was ninety-six when she died in 1928.

One of the things she told us was if we needed anything
— for example, to cut a tree for firewood or any other
useful purpose — we were to cut only what we needed.

Now, when we know and understand that leaves absorb
waste from the air, we understand this better. But — how
did she know and understand this?

When we were children, we were great ones for breaking
branches when we were out picking berries. To her and to
the Elders, everything was sacred. They had respect for
everything. When digging roots, she would first take
tobacco and place it where the root was. Then she would
take what she needed of the top or root and place the rest
back in the earth and cover it up. She would always put
back what was not needed.

Each tribe kept its own camp. When the head man or chief
went out hunting, they were only to take what they needed
— and not to waste anything. In that time, we were told
always to share.

I remember both my grandmother and my father saying,
"Even if you are hungry, if you know someone else needs
something, share what you have."

I always wonder how they came to know that there was
someone powerful looking after them, someone they could
pray to. Where did that knowledge come from? Who was
the Great Spirit who came to them?

They always said *Great Spirit* when speaking of God, and

they always said that they were to look after this land for the Great Spirit.

Which of the tribes of Israel are we from? Which of the tribes of Abraham are we? We are surely one of those.

I suppose it really doesn't matter since we are all children of Adam.

Jessie Saulteaux
Carry the Kettle,
Saskatchewan

Prayer for meditation
    . . . the land mourns,
   and all who live in it languish;
together with the wild birds and animals
   even the birds of the air,
   even the fish of the sea are
          perishing.
                    Hosea 4.3

Creator,
when we seek to serve you
with steadfast love,
your coming is as sure as the dawn.

You come to us like showers,
spring rains watering the earth.

With your strong arm you redeem your people,
leading your people like a flock.

You seek us — welcoming with open arms
all who turn to you.

May we serve you with gladness,
caring for those around us,
respecting the sacredness of all Creation.

173

Prayer for all people

That the grace of our Lord may overflow in us with the faith and love of Christ Jesus, let us pray to the Lord.

SUNDAY BETWEEN 18 AND 24 SEPTEMBER

You know the grace of our Lord Jesus Christ, that though he was rich, yet for your sake he became poor, so that by his poverty you might become rich. *2 Corinthians 8.9*

Readings

Hosea 11.1–11   *Psalm 107.1–9*
1 Timothy 2.1–7   *Luke 16.1–13*

I've always liked sewing.

When the children were little, they always wore what was made over. The Indian Agent used to give us old army surplus things to work with. I remember that when I had two young children, I made a beautiful suit for the boy and a skirt and jacket for the girl.

Others made quilts. We had a way of making quilts so that we put our names on them. We called them friendship quilts.

The Indian Agent asked if he could send two quilts and the outfits I had made for my children to Ottawa — just to let them see what we were doing. He told us that we would have these things returned to us. We never did see them again — although he did give us more materials so we could make more.

During the summer, when the berries were ripening, there were opportunities to go to the school and can berries. There was a person there who showed us how to do canning. Whatever we picked, we could put up in the basement of the school. This was during the summer holidays. I also liked to make jelly from the berries. If you are making jelly from the cherries, you need to make it in the first week that they're ripening — otherwise, it doesn't gel as well. Pin cherries make the best jelly. Sometimes people would give us some crab apples and they make a good jelly also. Sauce could also be made of this and we found we could make it very well and it was good.

For the last two years I have been unable to tighten the jars, so I have had to give up canning and jelly making.

Up to the 1940s we really couldn't travel anywhere. If you wanted to go anywhere, to go off the reserve for any reason, to see anyone, or to visit, you had to get a permit. There were lots of reasons for going off the reserve — but you always needed a permit. Also, if anyone wanted to come to the reserve — they needed a permit as well. The longest one could stay anywhere, even with a permit, was a month.

I learned about serving and leadership in school. But, I remember it was a man's job in the Indian way to serve and handle the sweetgrass and smudging the Pipe with sweetgrass in a ceremony. In a ceremony, everyone sat in a circle, and when they started a meeting, they began by following the sun in the circle. This meant that there was a place for everyone. This did not mean that they *had* to talk. It was so that each person felt that there was a place for them — and if they wished to speak they were invited to speak and felt they had a place in the circle.

Jessie Saulteaux
Carry the Kettle, Saskatchewan

Prayer for meditation

Creator,
you satisfy the thirsty
and fill the hungry with good things.

We pray for those who
find it hard to honour your word.

You have held us in your arms
and led us in kindness.

We give thanks for opportunities to serve in small ways,
knowing that our faithfulness in small matters
shows we live in the light of your love.

We give thanks for your love which endures forever.

Prayer for all people

That those in positions of authority may come to the truth
so that all may lead quiet and peaceable lives in godliness
and dignity, let us pray to the Lord.

SUNDAY BETWEEN 25 SEPTEMBER AND 1 OCTOBER

You know the grace of our Lord Jesus Christ, that though
he was rich, yet for your sake he became poor, so that by
his poverty you might become rich. *2 Corinthians 8.9*

Readings

Joel 2.23–30   Psalm 107.1, 33–43
1 Timothy 6.6–19   Luke 16.19–31

I was born and brought up in northern Ontario. My early
years were at Big Trout Lake and then later my parents
moved to Bearskin Lake. When I was seven years old my

parents were pressured into sending me to the Anglican Residential School at Pelican Lake near Sioux Lookout. It was far away from home and only accessible by plane from Big Trout Lake. After I left home for the first time, it was two years before I saw my parents again.

I was angry when I got home again after two years. One day my father sat me down and asked me why I was so angry. I pleaded with my father not to make me go back to Pelican School. I told him about all the bad things at the school and about how mean the staff at the school were to us.

My father asked me if I could say one good thing about the school. I told him I had made some friends and how one teacher was always trying to be nice to the children at the school.

I will always remember what my father said to me. He said, ''I know it must be hard for you. It is not easy to send you away to school, to go and live with strangers in a different world. It is very important for you to remember this thought. Always try to look for something good, no matter how small, in people who hurt you. Whatever happens, don't let your anger at them get the best of you.''

My father then pointed at my heart and said, ''If you get ugly thoughts in your heart it will show in your face. Don't let your face become ugly.''

I have never forgotten those words of my father.

It will be three years in November since my father died. Before he died, he told me that after the plane took me and my brother away to school, he would go by himself into the bush and would cry and pray for us in his sadness.

Phyllis Keeper
Winnipeg, Manitoba/
Big Trout Lake, Ontario

Prayer for meditation

Your sons and your daughters shall
    prophesy,
your old men shall dream dreams,
and your young men shall see visions.

Joel 3.28

Creator,
you are with us.
When we are alone, angry, and lashing out —
may we find rest in your love.

We give thanks for parents
who love and teach their children
with an understanding that guides them through their lives.

May we grow in wisdom and truth,
in the light of your steadfast love.

Prayer for all people

That we may take hold of the eternal truths of God, pursuing righteousness, godliness, faith, love, endurance, and gentleness, let us pray to the Lord.

SUNDAY BETWEEN 2 AND 8 OCTOBER

The word of the Lord abides for ever. That word is the good news which was preached to you. *1 Peter 1.25*

Readings

Amos 5.6–7, 10–15   *Psalm 101*
2 Timothy 1.1–14   *Luke 17.5–10*

My sister was a good help to me and we lived close together. When our husbands were away, and we needed food for our children, we sometimes set snares for rabbits

— and we set snares for rabbits in the fall when they were fat. Sometimes we could go to our mother-in-law for help. My sister did a lot to help when there were problems — although she had her own problems. She was beaten often. I don't know why he did that.

At my wedding, I made my own dress. Different ones gave us a little and we had a few things we needed from our father. Usually we got help with what we needed.

I have been married for fifty-seven years in 1990. The things I needed to know, getting married, getting children, how to look after a home, we learned from my grand-mother and later my sister helped me.

Over the years I was a midwife, and I helped when the babies were born and tended to the sick and people came to me to dress the bodies when they died. I remember going to my mother-in-law's house where the sister of my husband, a girl of about eighteen was dying. When we got there the girl told her mother to give us lunch and she was OK. After we finished lunch, she called her mother and said, "I'm going to sleep now, Mom." And she closed her eyes and took her last breath. The house was so small I wasn't far away. I had to wash her face and change her clothes for the wake and funeral. At that time they used to make their own box and line it with blankets and a pillow.

Jessie Saulteaux,
Carry the Kettle,
Saskatchewan

Prayer for meditation
Seek the Lord, and live.

Amos 5.6

Lord,
you are with us as we walk with sadness and grief.

Stretch out your hand
and look upon us with favour.

Grant that we may not be ashamed of trusting in you,
but guard the treasure of faith
entrusted to us through Jesus Christ our Lord.

Prayer for all people
That we may live with a sincere faith, rekindling the gift of
God in us who gives us a spirit of power and of love, let
us pray to the Lord.

SUNDAY BETWEEN 9 AND 15 OCTOBER

Give thanks in all circumstances, for this is the will of God
in Christ Jesus for you. *1 Thessalonians 5.18*

Readings
Micah 1.2; 2.1–10   *Psalm 26*
2 Timothy 2.8–15   *Luke 17.11–19*

Thanksgiving in Canada falls on the same day as Columbus
Day celebrations in many parts of the world. For Aboriginal
peoples, the coming to this country of Europeans meant
death — either by wars, forced labour, or disease. For
others it meant displacement and forced moves — often to
different places, places where it was difficult for them to
live in the way they had been accustomed.

For all, the coming of Europeans to this country marked an
end to a way of life that we had known for centuries. Our
communities are still facing the challenges which the confrontation between cultures has brought.

There is a prophesy within the Aboriginal Traditional community that there will be a second opportunity to make

things right between Aboriginal people and newcomers to this country.

I believe that we have that opportunity now. If we miss the opportunity now, we might not have another chance. There are many gifts in the Aboriginal community. We have to bring them forward, to offer them to the wider Church and also to our Aboriginal brothers and sisters internationally.

Some of our people have had the opportunity to travel. We have been to Australia and to parts of Central and South America. We know that some of our brothers and sisters are proclaiming the gospel of Christ at the risk of their lives. Their families and children are suffering. We have to join in solidarity with them.

Here, we need to struggle with what it is to serve God. Within our own Aboriginal community, there are disagreements. For some, a recovery of some parts of Aboriginal spirituality is absolutely necessary. For others, there are serious concerns about using any part of Native spirituality.

In my own family, my brother and I both were interested in spiritual things. We both entered United Church Seminary. He is now a Native Traditional Leader — and I continued in ministry in the United Church. We respect each other's ways.

We have to encourage each other. We have to be honest. We have to find our own way to the truth. We have to continue the dialogue.

One of the gifts given to the Church is the word. Words are very powerful and sometimes words are used in the wrong way. Words of the Bible are then not honoured.

If one uses words for power, then the words are not used in the right way. We must use words in a humble way.

The spirit provided us with the word. We must be careful and caring in words we use.

I am blessed to be Anishnabe. I find it hard to speak. It is easier for me to listen. To be teachers, we must first be listeners. Once we have been listeners, then we can talk.

We must learn to work and walk together with the larger Church and we must look to making our contributions to the international community. We have many gifts to offer.

Alf Dumont
Winnipeg, Manitoba/
Shawanaga, Ontario

Prayer for meditation
Vindicate me, O Lord,
    for I have walked in my integrity,
    and I have trusted in the Lord
       without wavering.
Prove me, O Lord, and try me;
    test my heart and mind.
For your steadfast love is before my eyes,
    and I walk in faithfulness with you.
Psalm 26.1–3

Creator,
your desire is that we live in peace.

Your call is to justice.
May we help those in need and speak against injustice,
walking uprightly in the knowledge of your love for all.

May we serve you with gladness and joy,
speaking the truth in love,
showing care and integrity to all.

Prayer for all people
That we may comprehend the word of God is not chained and avoid wrangling over words, continuing faithful and loving in proclaiming the truth, let us pray to the Lord.

183

SUNDAY BETWEEN 16 AND 22 OCTOBER

The word of God is living and active; it sifts the thoughts and intentions of the heart. *Hebrews 4.12*

Readings
Habakkuk, 1.1–3; 2.1–4   Psalm 119.137–144
2 Timothy, 3.14–4.5   Luke 18.1–8

There was a potato patch on the reserve. It was a patch that everyone worked on. Each person had their own place in it — but you weren't supposed to pick any potatoes until a certain time in August. I remember once talking to my brother-in-law. It was after a rain and there was not much to eat on the reserve. My brother-in-law said that he thought he would go to the potato patch and get some potatoes; it was soon enough for the potatoes — but we weren't supposed to pick them until the farm inspector said so. He said "I can pick them in the night — and with the rain washing away the tracks, no-one is going to catch me!"

I remembered that all my life. It wasn't the potatoes, whether someone would catch him at that; that didn't really matter and I can't remember if he got caught stealing his own potatoes. But I remember telling him, "There's someone watching over us. Someone is sure to be seeing us in everything we do, in every part of our lives."

The 23rd Psalm and 1 Corinthians 13 are what I have really lived with. I have met a lot of different people in different ways. Sometimes people talk about others in bad ways. But there is something in the verses which is very strong and tells us of the love we should have for one another. Even if people talk about me, I can't hate them. These passages and all the other little passages I learned when a child have really helped me through life.

When our family were young, we saw that they were baptized. Sometimes it was two weeks and sometimes it

184

was a month after they were born, but we saw to it that they were baptized before they were grown up — although they only had church services once a month. Sometimes the student ministers came to us from May to September — and when they came, they always seemed to come to me for advice on 'what they were supposed to do. Many times I had my own problems but I always had a way to get over them knowing that God, that Christ will carry the load. Christ will carry the problems.

I believe that when we pray and ask Christ to take our load, he does. I don't think, though, that prayer is answered right away. It is strange sometimes the way that prayer is answered.

Jessie Saulteaux
Carry the Kettle, Saskatchewan

Prayer for meditation
You are righteous, O Lord.
We delight in your ways.

In your love, hear our voices,
our cries to you for help.

The wisdom of Elders teaches
that your will gorws when we pray
and live by your word.

Lord, we wait in stillness,
trusting you are there, you will answer.

Lord, help us carry the load.

Prayer for all people
That we may continue what we have learned and firmly believed since childhood, being persistent and patient in proclaiming the gospel through good times and bad, let us pray to the Lord.

SUNDAY BETWEEN 23 AND 29 OCTOBER

God was in Christ reconciling the world to himself, and he
has entrusted us with the message of reconciliation.
2 Corinthians 5.19

Readings
Zephaniah 3.1–9   Psalm 3
2 Timothy 4.6–8, 16–18   Luke 18.9–14

I put aside Traditional ways because when I went to residential school, they told me it was a sin to go to sun-
dances. For a long time I hated the people who told us
those things. They slapped us left and right if they found
out we had gone to a sundance ceremony.

Today, we have been given the apology by the United
Church of Canada. I was one of the ones that suffered. So
many of those years were wasted. I had another way to go
because my mother always went to church.

When the Sacred Fire is burned, when the Sacred Bundle
is opened, these are very special times. It is like a jewelry
box — this is how the Elders treat the Sacred Bundle.

When God gave us his Son, Jesus Christ, there were three
wise men. These men were like our Elders — and they
brought gifts: incense. Incense is like our sweetgrass — a
nice-smelling thing.

I have a bracelet — and on my bracelet, I have sweetgrass
— to carry with me also the Traditional way. God made
me an Indian — but I can say, I am truly a Christian also
and so I also carry a cross on my bracelet. God gave me a
heart. I have a little drum here on my bracelet as well. This
drum beats like my heart beats. It is a symbol that people
who are sick may be healed.

The feather I carry is the feather of the eagle that we
cherish in the Bible. The eagle has strong wings. God gave

me the eagle for a purpose: I pray and the prayers will be taken on strong wings to God.

When Christ died, he died on the cross for the remission of sins; when he died on the cross, he died for the remission of *my* sins. I carry this piece of red wool; it represents to me his blood.

These Traditional ways are to be cherished, the Elders tell us. Let's start from here. Let's listen to the Elders.

The Sacred Fire is a living fire — and water is also living. God says — this is living water. Red water resembles the blood of Christ and is shed for you and for me so our sins are forgiven.

We are all Indian even though some of us don't understand. When God comes to judge, does he have to talk in English? Learn your own language.

Edith Memnook
Goodfish Lake, Alberta

Prayer for meditation
You, O Lord, are a shield
    around me,
my glory, and the one who lifts up my head.
Psalm 3.3

Creator,
show us your countenance,
lead us to your holy place.

We give thanks for Elders
who bring healing and guide the way to reconciliation
using symbols which we know in our lives.

Prayer for all people

That we may keep the faith to the end of our time trusting in the strength of the Lord always, let us pray to the Lord.

SUNDAY BETWEEN 30 OCTOBER TO 5 NOVEMBER

God so loved the world that he gave his only Son, that whoever believes in him should not perish but have eternal life. *John 3.16*

Readings

Haggai 2.1–9   *Psalm 65.1–8*
2 Thessalonians 1.5–12   *Luke 19.1–10*

In my community we are matrilineal, and so teachings are transmitted by the mothers and grandmothers. My grandmother has taught me many things, and I love to be with her. Here is how she teaches.

Once I was working on a summer project in my community. While we were working, my grandmother came and told the people I work with that she needed me. No one would question the authority of my grandmother and so I was excused from work. I found out that she needed me for berry picking!

We went out picking berries away — away up a hill — and I could see the village a far way off in the distance. After we had picked for some time she said to me, "We must go back now; you must lead the way." I said, "But I can't." She said, "You can — I will follow you!" So I began to walk through the thick bush and she kept on following me. She never corrected me or told me which way to go — only followed everywhere I went in all the ways I was lost and never ever said anything. This was taking a

long time and soon I knew it would be dark so I said again, "Grandmother, I can't do this."

She replied, "Oh, yes, you can . . . . go ahead!" The sun was beginning to set and it was growing dark and I was more and more worried. I came to a very steep and mossy hill and I said again. "Grandmother, I can't do this. Look, we can't go down this hill!" She said, "Oh yes we can!" — and together we went sliding and laughing down that long, mossy hill. I will never forget the way that she laughed and laughed.

I did find our way back but it took a very long time and all the time the berries we carried grew heavier. I thought it would have been much easier if she had just told me how to get down the hill since she knew the way. But she would not tell me. She wanted me to learn the lesson of how to watch where I was going and to take note of the way that we were going. This was her way of teaching me — and it is a lesson I never forgot!

Monica McKay
Toronto, Ontario/Greenville, British Columbia

Prayer for meditation
You make the gateways of the
    morning and the evening
    shout for joy.
                 Psalm 8

Creator, we delight in the love, humour, and wisdom
of those who love us and show the way we should live.
We give thanks for laughter and fun.

Like the prophets of old,
you call us to build your holy temple on earth.
You work through our hands and hearts.

191

We give thanks for the saints before us
who have kept faith and have shown us the way to life.

May we live and serve with gladness.

Prayer for all people
That God will make us worthy of his call and fulfill by his power every good resolve and work of faith, let us pray to the Lord.

SUNDAY BETWEEN 6 AND 12 NOVEMBER

Jesus Christ is the first-born of the dead; to him be glory and dominion for ever and ever. *See Revelation 1.5,6*

Readings
Zechariah 7.1–10	*Psalm 9.11–20*
2 Thessalonians 2.13–3.5	*Luke 20.27–38*

I am Cree.

In my community, there has been a custom in the past for parents to arrange the marriages of their children. This was sometimes done for all the wrong reasons because sometimes it was because a man was a good hunter or a woman was a good worker. This often created great problems because people would sometimes marry when they didn't even like each other. The people would sometimes get along and learn to love — and the love would grow.

At other times there was great hardship. But people could sometimes accept this, overcome the difficulties, and understand God's commandment and keep the commitment, and love would grow.

192

I have four children. The first two married because they had children. There was a lot of pressure from the community for them to marry — and we as parents also felt that they should marry. Therefore, we tried our best to help. We understood that they would have problems but my wife and I were in a position to try to help them — and so we did the best that we could by sharing our own problems and how to deal with them.

Our second youngest daughter is now eighteen and she is going steady now for some time. In the community there is now a feeling that they have been going together long enough and that they should get married.

Since they are both over eighteen, I feel that they should make up their own minds . . . on their own. I have talked to them. I have told them that I love them both. They are saying that they would like to get married — but not right now.

There is community pressure. As a father, I feel it would be wrong to force them to get married. Even though they say they intend to get married, I would have a very difficult time with my conscience if I were to see my daughter at the altar knowing she were not feeling that this is the right time for her to be married. Then perhaps there would be some resentment or feelings about this. Above all, she might not be ready for marriage.

So, I do not follow the custom of old — and I respect the wishes of my daughter.

David Masty
Whapmagoostui (Great Whale River), Quebec

Prayer for meditation
Creator,
your prophets called on all to render true judgements —
showing kindness and mercy to one another.

193

May we stand firm in your grace,
nourishing and deepening our faith
understanding that you are the God of the living
and you call us to fuller life.

We give thanks for the love of a parent
who has courage to look at the ways of old
and in the light of your love, find a new way.

We give thanks for all those in positions of leadership,
asking that your hand be continually upon them
that they may seek your wisdom and truth in all matters.

Prayer for all people
That the Lord may comfort our hearts and direct us to the
love of God and the steadfastness of Christ, let us pray to
the Lord.

SUNDAY BETWEEN 13 AND 19 NOVEMBER

Look up and raise your heads, because your redemption is
drawing near. *Luke 21.28*

Readings
Malachi 4.1–6   Psalm 82
2 Thessalonians 3.6–13   Luke 21.5–19

When you look at a tree, you will notice that for every year
it survives, there is a circle. The next year another forms —
and the year after, there is another. Eventually, the tree
becomes strong.

The medicine wheel is like a tree. In the medicine wheel
are the four directions — the east, the south, the west,
and the north. The medicine wheel teaches us a holistic
approach to life.

Knowledge of ourselves as human beings is a protection for us, a help to how we live. We must understand the medicine wheel to bring healing to ourselves and to our communities.

All learning is on a path beginning in the east. The east is called the place of *illumination*. This is a simple word meaning "seeing." Illumination represents physical sight as well as spiritual insight — the way of the soul.

South is where warmth comes from. This is the place of growth; we keep on growing — we never reach a place where we stop. *Trust and innocence*, accepting our humanness, become foremost in our minds as we journey through the place represented by south on the medicine wheel. Sometimes we judge each other too harshly; we need to learn to be kind, to accept ourselves.

The west is a place of *introspection*. Here we learn to look at ourselves. It is important to be able to look at ourselves, to see within. It is much easier to judge others — but we need to evaluate ourselves, to know our own humanity.

Knowledge begins in the north. We can never start by seeing something and knowing. We must always start by seeing how something works. All learning takes time and work.

The more we understand about life, the deeper our roots grow. We must keep in balance these four things: illumination, trust and innocence, introspection, and knowledge. As we understand these things, moving in circles outward, always growing, always learning, we will become strong like the tree — the tree of life.

God works through people. People who are spiritually strong have a glow — a love of life. These are our Elders, the people who bring healing in our communities. They do not seek to gain personal power. Instead, they are kind people,

channels for the healing which is carried out by the
Creator.

William Dumas
Thompson/South Indian Lake
Manitoba

Prayer for meditation

The sun of righteousness shall rise,
    with healing in its wings.
                            Malachi 4.2

Creator,
we give thanks for teachings
which help us to know how to live.

May we set our eyes upon you
looking always for ways to serve,
bringing healing to our communities.

Lord, give us your words and your wisdom
that we may be instruments of your peace.

Prayer for all people

That we may do our work quietly and diligently, and not
weary of doing good, let us pray to the Lord.

LAST SUNDAY AFTER PENTECOST:
THE REIGN OF CHRIST

Blessed is he who comes in the name of the Lord! Blessed
is the kingdom of our father David that is coming.
Mark 11.9, 10

Readings

2 Samuel 5.1–5   Psalm 95
Colossians 1.11–20   John 12.9–19

I was in the military, serving in Germany on a peace-keeping mission on Christmas Eve.

Some of us went out for a drink. We saw there two young German soldiers about our age. We had seen them many times without talking to them. One of them was a tall, blond man — a beautiful-looking guy.

I was always self-conscious about myself from the time I was little. I was skinny. When I stood sideways, you could hardly see a shadow. I hated being small.

Sometimes, I'd try to stand up tall and hide my bow-legs. But, the sergeant would come by and say ''Oh, for heaven's sake Anderson — you're going to fall over if you stay like that for long.'' So I'd relax — and my legs would bow again. I've always felt self-conscious about my looks.

Well, we looked at these soldiers. We didn't usually mix — but we thought, ''Ah, what the heck — it's Christmas!'' We invited them over to our table. When we were sitting there, we were laughing and telling stories.

I was telling them about what it was like back home on the reserve with all of us kids fooling around and playing tricks on each other. We never had very much, poor as could be — but we had a lot of fun.

The tall beautiful guy told us his name was Hans. He was just looking at us. All of a sudden he said, ''I wish I had a family.''

We all looked at him. We didn't know what to say. He explained that he had been born during the war in an experimental camp. He never knew either of his parents or if he had any relatives.

197

After a long pause I said, "I know what we'll do Hans!
We'll adopt you." He started to cry. I'll never forget that.
He just broke down and cried and couldn't stop.

After that, we always talked when we saw each other.
Before we left Germany, we became quite good friends.

Art Anderson
Regina/Kāneonuskatēw, Saskatchewan

Prayer for meditation
Creator,
in your hand are the depths of the earth,
and the height of the mountains.
The sea is yours and your hands prepared the land.
You created the heavens and the earth,
and hold everything together.

You have rescued us from darkness
and delivered us into the Kingdom of your Son.

Through your Son, Christ,
we are reconciled to you in heaven and on earth,
by making peace through his death on the cross.

We praise your holy name,
giving thanks to you always
for your covenant of love.

May we extend love and mercy
to the ends of the earth,
to those who have been our enemies,
in unexpected places.

Prayer for all people
That we may be strong in the Lord, joyfully giving thanks
to the Father who has enabled us to share in the inheritance of saints in the light, let us pray to the Lord.

Contributors

First Nations Ecumenical Liturgical Resources Board

Joyce Carlson is a writer and social worker with an interest in community development. Her childhood was in a rural family with connections in the early Red River Anglican as well as United churches. Joyce is Anglican and active in her diocese. With roots in the Métis, Scots, British and Swedish cultures, she is firmly committed to creative cross-cultural communication. Joyce edits a quarterly newsletter for the Dr. Jessie Saulteaux Resource Centre.

The Reverend Alf Dumont, Speaker of the All Native Circle Conference, grew up on the edge of Shawanaga, near Nobel, Ontario. A graduate of Emmanuel Theological College, he has served congregations in Toronto and Southern Ontario and worked in Australia before being appointed the first Director of the Dr. Jessie Saulteaux Resource Centre in 1984. Alf became Speaker of the All Native Circle Conference at its inception in 1988.

The Reverend Laverne Jacobs, National Coordinator of the Council for Native Ministries for the Anglican Church of Canada, studied at Huron College, Ontario. Laverne grew up on Walpole Island Reserve. He worked in a bank for a number of years in Wallaceburg before following his call into the ministry. He served in parishes on Walpole Island, Forest, and Kettle Point for thirteen years before joining the staff of the National Office of the Anglican church in 1987.

The Most Reverend Walter Jones, Archbishop of the Diocese of Rupert's Land and Metropolitan of the Ecclesiastical Province of Rupert's Land served in the positions of priest and administrator in Manitoba and South Dakota for twenty years before being consecrated Bishop of South Dakota on Pine Ridge Reservation in 1970. He was elected Bishop of Rupert's Land in 1983. He was given the name *Gnugnishka* meaning "grasshopper" by the Standing Bear family and *Tisiwasu* meaning "tall pine" by the Lambert family.

The Reverend Dr. Stan McKay is Director of the Dr. Jessie Saulteaux Resource Centre, a United Church Aboriginal Theological Centre. Stan studied education and taught two years before returning to university to study theology. He served congregations in Manitoba, then joined the National Church staff as coordinator of Native Ministries in 1982, there guiding the formation of the All Native Circle Conference. Appointed to his present position in 1988, Stan is a Pipe Carrier in the Native Tradition and holds an Honorary Doctorate from United Theological Seminary/McGill University.

Artist

Teresa Altiman is an Ojibwe artist who has studied at the Ontario College of Art, graduating in 1971. She subsequently received a fellowship from the College. She is best known for her silk screen prints. Her art has been published in teaching materials for schools aimed at developing understanding of Aboriginal culture and language. Teresa travels widely, has published art cards, and entered work in art shows. Teresa is employed as an editor by the Walpole Island First Nations Council. She has received an Eagle Feather from her community.

200